PAUL AXELROD

The Promise of Schooling: Education in Canada, 1800–1914

UNIVERSITY OF TORONTO PRESS
Toronto Buffalo London

D1208243

© University of Toronto Press Incorporated 1997
Toronto Buffalo London

Printed in Canada

Reprinted 1999

ISBN 0-8020-0825-9 (cloth)
ISBN 0-8020-7815-x (paper)

Printed on acid-free paper

Canadian Cataloguing in Publication Data

Axelrod, Paul Douglas
  The promise of schooling

  (Themes in Canadian social history)
  Includes bibliographical references and index.
  ISBN 0-8020-0825-9 (bound).   ISBN 0-8020-7815-x (pbk.)

  1. Education – Canada – History – 19th century.
  I. Title.   II. Series.

  LA411.7.A93 1997   370'.971'09034   C96-932435-9

University of Toronto Press acknowledges the financial
assistance to its publishing program of the Canada
Council and the Ontario Arts Council.

THEMES IN CANADIAN SOCIAL HISTORY

Editors: Craig Heron and Franca Iacovetta

THE PROMISE OF SCHOOLING: EDUCATION IN CANADA, 1800–1914

The Promise of Schooling explores the links between social and educational change in the complex and dynamic period between 1800 and 1914, when Canadian society and its school systems were forged. It raises and seeks to answer a number of questions: How extensive was schooling in the early nineteenth century? What lay behind the campaign to extend publicly funded education? What went on inside the Canadian classroom? How did schools address the needs of Native students, blacks, and the children of immigrants? What cultural and social roles did universities serve by the beginning of the twentieth century? And how were schools affected by the economic and social pressures arising from the Industrial Revolution?

The book contends that educational authorities built and reformed schools in ways that were not always consistent with their idealistic visions. Economic constraints, political expediency, and the agendas of ordinary citizens all influenced the life of the Canadian school in an era marked by dynamic social change.

Drawing from an abundant scholarly literature published over the last two decades, this study seeks to expose readers to the richness of the field of educational history. Written for a broad audience, it also hopes, by providing historical context, to stimulate informed discussion about educational issues.

(Themes in Canadian Social History)

Paul Axelrod is a professor in the Division of Social Science at York University. His previous publications include *Making a Middle Class: Student Life in Canadian Universities during the Thirties* and *Scholars and Dollars: Politics, Economics, and the Universities of Ontario, 1945–1980*.

Contents

Preface

Virtually all young Canadians today embark upon a program of extended schooling, but this was not always the case. In the early nineteenth century, only a minority of young people registered to be students in formal schools, and even fewer attended school on a regular basis. While some schools were publicly subsidized, most depended upon tuition-fee income and private sponsorship in order to survive. By the beginning of the twentieth century, Canada's educational landscape had been dramatically transformed. Publicly funded, free elementary schooling was now the norm, and the majority of young people were sent to school because the law – and their parents – required them to attend. Secondary schooling, though still inaccessible to most adolescents at that time, would eventually become a regular part of their educational experience. While universities would continue to serve a select constituency, their intellectual and social roles had also been notably modified by the turn of the century.

This book attempts to describe and account for major developments in the history of Canadian schooling up to the beginning of the First World War. It raises and seeks to answer a number of questions. How extensive was schooling in the early nineteenth century? What lay behind the campaign to extend publicly funded education? What went on inside the Canadian classroom? How did schools address the needs of Native students, blacks, and the children of immigrants? What cultural and social roles did universities serve by the beginning of the twentieth century? How were schools affected by the economic and social pressures arising from the Industrial Revolution?

In previous generations, the 'story' of Canadian schooling, from the elementary to the post-secondary levels, was told simply and enthusiastically. Educational visionaries, committed to the scholarly enrichment of their communities, championed the cause of public schooling. Their unstinting efforts bore fruit, and by the end of the nineteenth century, several years of formal education had become the norm for Canadian youth, a prerequisite for the continuing progress of society and the enlightenment of its population.

This study contends that the traditional account of the development of schooling in Canada is not so much incorrect as incomplete. The growth of public schooling should be understood not only as the product of individual enterprise, but as the result of social changes that swept through society in the nineteenth century. As they directed educational policy, school promoters were themselves shaped by the environment in which they lived. The schools they sponsored sometimes encouraged change and sometimes resisted it. This book explores the social context in which educational policy was formed and implemented. It probes, too, the unanticipated consequences and limitations of educational reform.

This study also pays attention to some educational players who were not commonly included in earlier historical accounts focusing on the ideas and accomplishments of educational-policy makers. Parents, teachers, and students also sought, and at times played, an important role in shaping the life of schools and universities. The relations between them and educational authorities were dynamic and complex, and this volume hopes to capture something of that interaction.

Women, visible minorities, and ethnic communities were all affected by educational changes introduced in the nineteenth and early twentieth centuries. But they were perceived and treated differently from other students in the educational mainstream. Even as schooling became available to more and more Canadians, gaps remained between the opportunities available to the relatively privileged and to the less advantaged. As they do in other areas of Canadian social history, the themes of gender and social class figure prominently in the annals of Canadian education.

Indeed, as readers will quickly discover, this book is indebted to the work of other historians. In the past two decades, scholarly research in the history of Canadian education has flourished. With energy and sophistication, academics have explored various aspects of this subject from a variety of perspectives, and this book aims to expose readers to the richness of the published literature. Many, though by no means all, of the scholars in the field are mentioned in this text, which also, on occasion, attempts to give readers a flavour of the historiographical debates that have informed their work. Virtually every theme raised in this book merits more exploration than the space available here has allowed, and I hope that those who are so inspired will pursue their study of these subjects. References listed at the end of the book ought to prove helpful in this regard.

Much of the 'new' educational history has a regional or provincial focus. Case-studies of educational development tend to highlight the unique features of Canada's provincial educational systems. Work on the history of Upper Canada and Ontario in the nineteenth century has been especially abundant in recent years, and, as a synthesis of the literature, *The Promise of Schooling* reflects this historiographical orientation. This book is certainly attuned to regional differences in the history of education, but it stresses common patterns of development in an attempt to present a 'Canadian' school experience.

Aside from acknowledging generally my fellow historians

from whose work I have liberally drawn, I want to identify the contributions of particular individuals. I thank Wyn Millar and Robert Gidney not only for their comments on the draft manuscript, but also for their exemplary scholarship in the history of education. Gerald Hallowell from the University of Toronto Press shared both his enthusiasm and his editorial expertise. Etta Baichman provided valuable research assistance. I am especially grateful to the co-editor of this series, Craig Heron, for his encouragement and sound advice. As colleagues and friends for nearly three decades, Craig and I are co-veterans and survivors of many educational struggles, including the completion of this book. Two other friends, Paul Anisef and Ken Hundert, have guided and assisted me in ways that are not merely academic. So too have my immediate and extended families. My deepest debt is to Susan Friedman and our daughter, Kaitlyn, who inspire and enrich me every day of my life. I dedicate this book to them, with love.

THE PROMISE OF SCHOOLING:
EDUCATION IN CANADA, 1800–1914

1

Schooling and the Community

In the early nineteenth century, schooling mattered to many British North American colonists, but sheer survival mattered more. Challenged by hostile weather, primitive modes of transportation, the relentless demands of farming or fishing, deadly diseases, and the eruption of war, people were preoccupied with living, and making a living. Children were not sheltered from these burdens and responsibilities. With their parents, they worked the land and cared for the household. When there was time, and if resources allowed, they might attend a 'common,' private, or denominational school in their area. Youth from relatively privileged families were the most likely to do so. Where they lacked the opportunity for formal learning, children, in the privacy of their homes, might be told Bible stories, and even taught how to read them. Both inside and outside the household, schooling and religion were closely linked. Gradually, the virtues of 'public' education were recognized, and throughout the colonies' towns and villages, state-funded schooling spread. This chapter explores the conditions which shaped education and its place in community life from the turn of the nineteenth century to the 1840s.

The territory now known as Canada was occupied in the early 1600s by some 300,000 Native people who spoke twelve major languages and numerous dialects. European explorers, traders, and missionaries soon brought to the 'new' world values and ambitions that clashed with those of the Native population. Intent on territorial expansion and commercial success, the French sought to pacify aboriginals through a combination of violence, alliance, and appeasement. Pioneering missionaries attempted to convert Natives to Catholicism, force them into non-migratory agricultural practices, teach them European customs and manners, and compel them to speak French. These efforts largely failed because they were utterly foreign to Native traditions and irrelevant to the people's daily needs. Reared in mainly nomadic families, and accustomed to permissive child-rearing practices, Indian children resented, and at times resisted, the rigid pedagogical approaches of boarding- and mission schools. European conceptions of time, competition, and private property could not be reconciled with the Native values of natural order and cooperation. While Native peoples were attracted by European technology and drawn into the economic system of the fur trade, they clung to their cultural traditions, even as they were gradually overwhelmed by the forces of immigration, settlement, and development. Institutionalized schooling controlled by others had little to offer them, though, as we shall see later, British and Canadian authorities would adopt a strategy intended, once again, to reshape and regulate Indian lives.

For its own children, the French regime had established a small network of 'petites écoles' which offered basic elementary education, primarily to boys, within a firmly religious framework. Totalling some forty-seven during the life of the regime, these were Canada's first formal schools. Ursuline nuns, who arrived at Quebec in 1639, provided schooling for a handful of the colony's girls, stressing biblical studies, domestic skills, needlework, and etiquette. The religious order the Congrégation de Notre-Dame, which opened a school in Montreal in 1657, assumed primary responsibility for the education of females, still prescribing a domestically oriented curriculum. Secondary and higher education, exclusively for males, was offered in the Jesuit Collège de Québec, established in 1635; the Grande Séminaire (1663); and the Petite Séminaire (1668). Middle- and upper-class youth seeking general classical training, or certification for the priesthood, attended these institutions. In addition, trade schools were opened at Quebec, Saint-Joachim, and Montreal, where skills such as carving, carpentry, masonry, surgery, and painting were taught. By 1760, estimated literacy rates in Quebec compared favourably with those in France, and unfavourably with those in the New England colonies. Colonists in rural parishes, many of which lacked schools, were the least literate. Poor weather, the requirements of farming, the lure of the fur trade, the shortage of teachers and books, and the inconsistent support shown schooling by the Church and Crown all inhibited the further development of education in New France. Still, significant initiatives in the training of boys and girls had been taken during the era of the French regime.

Following the Conquest of 1759, when the French were defeated by the English, the prospects for schooling were dim. A number of school buildings, including the Grande Séminaire of Quebec, had been wrecked by the war. Though the Quebec Act of 1774 permitted the survival of the Catholic religion and the French language, formal education languished. The Jesuit, Récollet, and Sulpician orders were forbidden by the government to recruit new priests, and by 1791 only eighteen Catholic clergy were involved in education in Lower Canada. The French-speaking population of 160,000 was now serviced by a mere forty schools, and secondary and post-secondary education virtually disappeared for several years. On the other hand, the female religious orders were allowed to enlist new teachers;

consequently girls were probably better educated than boys in the last part of the eighteenth century. Military defeat had been costly to French Canadians. How they and their schools would fare in the years ahead would depend on the relationships they forged with a government they mistrusted, a Church which sought to guide them, and an English-speaking community growing in their midst.

For all their cultural and linguistic differences, English and French colonists in the late eighteenth century shared these traits: their fate on the North American continent had been determined by war, and they lived in a world in which religion and schooling were deeply entwined. The American Revolution of 1776 led to the exodus of some 40,000 'Loyalists,' 30,000 of whom settled in Nova Scotia and New Brunswick, and some 8,000 in Quebec, which in 1791 was divided into the two provinces of Lower Canada and Upper Canada. Prepared to proclaim their loyalty to the British Crown, the newcomers had diverse backgrounds. Those of Scottish and English Protestant origin were accompanied by Black and Indian Loyalists, Germans, the Dutch, and Scottish Highland Catholics. Initially, the politically dominant among them were members of the Anglican Church, which sought to reproduce English values and customs in the Canadian colonies. The principles of conservatism, social hierarchy, monarchism, and anti-Americanism informed their beliefs, as did the notion of an established, privileged Church which would control education.

The Anglicans of Nova Scotia and New Brunswick gave substance to their convictions by founding King's College in Windsor, Nova Scotia, in 1789, and the College of New Brunswick (Fredericton) in 1800, which was renamed King's College in 1829. Modelled on Oxford University, but by no means as successful, these schools were expected to train Anglican clergymen, who would provide religious and moral leadership to their communities. Non-Anglicans were initially unwelcome, both as teachers and as students, in these institutions.

A similar attempt to establish a King's College in Upper Canada soon after the province was formed did not bear fruit for several decades, though the government did provide land which was used to secure an endowment for this project. In addition, British authorities reserved one-seventh of all Crown lands in Upper Canada for the 'support and maintenance of a Protestant Clergy,' which, in practice, meant the Church of England. This policy, which enhanced the powers and educational privileges of the Anglican Church at the expense of other religious denominations, was a continuing source of controversy through the early nineteenth century. Anglicans played a major role in founding grammar schools, which stressed the teaching of Latin and Greek, and which were intended to prepare youth for positions of occupational and social leadership in their communities. One such school was opened in 1803 in Cornwall by John Strachan, a prominent Anglican clergyman and educator, a tireless campaigner for King's College, and a leading proponent of state-funded education under the authority of the Church of England.

Throughout the eighteenth and early nineteenth centuries, a Church of England missionary organization, the Society for the Propagation of the Gospel (SPG), on the authority of the British Crown provided schooling to a portion of the Protestant populations of Nova Scotia, New Brunswick, and Newfoundland. In New Brunswick, the SPG, supported by the arrival of Loyalists from the United States, operated fourteen primary schools by 1800. In Upper Canada, there were nineteen schools in existence before the turn of the century, run by private proprietors or by religious denominations, not all of which were Anglican.

Indeed, throughout the colonies, Catholics and Protestant 'dissenters,' like the 'Planters' of Nova Scotia, who had emigrated from New England well before the American

Revolution, challenged the Anglican dominance in education along with other manifestations of the denomination's political privilege. Achieving numerical superiority and greater influence by the early nineteenth century, non-Anglicans would give new direction to colonial education.

From the 1790s to the end of the 1840s, close to 1 million immigrants arrived in British North America from the British Isles, an influx which increased and diversified the colonies' populations. By 1841 there were ten non-Natives for every aboriginal in a total population of more than 1.6 million. French-speaking peoples now numbered approximately 600,000, compared with nearly 1 million English. Probably half of the English-speaking immigrants were Irish; by the time of Confederation in 1867, they constituted the largest non-French ethnic group in British North America, with an especially prominent presence in Ontario, New Brunswick, Newfoundland, and non-francophone Quebec. Some 40 per cent of the Irish were Catholic, and 60 per cent were Protestant, made up of several denominational sects. Contrary to popular legend, which portrayed the typical Irish immigrant as a slum-dwelling, urban worker, the majority lived and worked in the Canadian countryside. The Catholic Irish, however, constituted a higher proportion of skilled and unskilled labourers than did their Protestant counterparts. Those emigrating to Canada in the wake of the disastrous Irish potato famine of the 1840s were generally poorer than their countrymen who had arrived earlier in the century.

Also drawn to Canada by the push of economic uncertainty and the lure of expected prosperity were Scottish immigrants, some 200,000 of whom were living in Nova Scotia by 1837. They were the largest immigrant group in Prince Edward Island; a significant presence in Quebec and

Ontario; and, on the initiative of Thomas Douglas, Earl of Selkirk, the founders (in 1811) of the Red River colony on the site of present-day Winnipeg.

Immigrants brought with them a diversity of cultural traditions that helped shape the religious and educational life of the British colonies. In Canada West (Ontario), for example, Church of England adherents constituted 22 per cent of the population in 1842, still the largest denomination. But their numbers were almost equalled and would soon be surpassed by Presbyterians and Methodists. The proportion of Catholics and, to a lesser degree, Baptists was also steadily growing in Ontario and elsewhere. Evangelicalism, a strain of Christianity adhered to by Methodists, Baptists, Congregationalists, and some Presbyterians, was a powerful presence in English Canada during much of the nineteenth century. Its followers believed in the individual's ability to forge a direct relationship with God, unmediated by the hierarchies, rituals, and creeds of the established (Anglican and Catholic) churches. Spiritual conversion could occur privately or in open-air revival meetings, led by lay preachers and infused with expressions of passion and emotionalism.

Canadian evangelicalism was generally more temperate than its 'radical' American equivalent. The political moderation of leaders like Methodist Egerton Ryerson, a prominent minister and educator in Ontario, and Presbyterian Thomas McCulloch, a Scottish-born scholar and teacher in Nova Scotia, enhanced the respectability and appeal of their respective movements. In an era when educational initiatives were inspired frequently by religious commitment, the authority that such individuals commanded affected the success of the projects they favoured. McCulloch established Pictou Academy in 1816, an institution designed both to prepare Presbyterian clergy and to offer a liberal education to other Christian students. Supported by the elected House of Assembly, Pictou faced opposition from conservative forces in the non-elected 'Council of Twelve,' and from traditionalists in McCulloch's own church who mistrusted his more liberal theology. The college closed in 1831, but McCulloch's campaign for higher education continued. He became the first president of the non-sectarian, though Presbyterian-oriented, Dalhousie College in Halifax. Ryerson was the founding principal of Victoria College in Cobourg, Ontario, which began as a Methodist academy in 1832 and became a university in 1842. Over the next two decades, Catholics, Baptists, Presbyterians, and Anglicans established additional academies and colleges, a number of which became full-fledged universities. Throughout the colonies, righteous educators competed for the souls and minds of a diverse and growing population, and schooling was a vital element in this campaign.

Religious instruction, and the assumed moral training it embodied, was thus one motivation for parents to seek formal schooling for their children. In addition, well-off families occupying leading social positions in their communities hoped that élite schooling would help secure their children's social status in the future. Boys, destined for the professions or government service, would receive classical education at a Canadian private school; a grammar school (the forerunner of the public secondary school); or a 'superior' academic institution in France, Britain, or the United States. Girls from middle-class backgrounds were less likely than boys to receive formal education, but those who did were instructed by private tutors, or in female 'academies,' where they were taught academic and cultural subjects designed to equip them with knowledge and skills considered appropriate to their gender and class.

Such opportunities were beyond the reach of struggling farmers and workers, but their interest in 'common' schooling, which offered a rudimentary, 'plain' English education, gradually grew. Literate children would at least be able to read the Bible, a skill valued by families irrespective of their social class. Schooled children might earn greater respect among their peers, and schools themselves, like churches, could help foster a sense of community for families otherwise isolated in frontier settings.

However deep their devotion to the cause, schooling enthusiasts faced major obstacles in the early nineteenth century. Historian Graeme Wynn characterizes British North American society as 'rough, ready, vigorous and violent. Life was hard and dangerous. Death was a frequent, unexpected visitor. Sudden storms, crashing trees, unstable canoes, malfunctioning machinery, dysentery, disease and the perils of childbirth ended many young lives.' In this challenging environment, survival was the priority.

The work which occupied most Canadians was hazardous and demanding, and rarely required much formal schooling. Farmers, fishers, fur traders, foresters, canal builders, and road workers learned their trades on the job. So did blacksmiths, saddlers, and boot makers, who acquired their skills through long apprenticeships with master craftsmen. Government officials, merchants, doctors, lawyers, and clergymen were more likely to have been formally educated, a benefit they would normally seek to extend to their children. Edward Arthur, the son of a lieutenant-governor of Upper Canada, attended the élite Upper Canada College before being sent to study in England. He returned to Canada and worked for his father in the lieutenant-governor's office. By contrast, Joseph Montferrand (b. 1802), the son of a Quebec voyageur, learned the shorter catechism from his sister; never attended school; and became a boxer, a logger, and, like his father, a voyageur.

Because most Canadians farmed, and because farming was a family enterprise, child labour was a normal part of the British North American life-course. Set to work at age seven or eight, boys would help with the sowing and reaping, graduating when they were older to heavier jobs such as driving horses, ploughing, and construction. Young girls would be responsible for feeding the animals and caring for siblings. Later they would learn from their mothers how to make clothes, prepare meals, and clean the farmhouse. Spring and fall – the planting and harvesting seasons – required everyone's labour.

Children had more 'free' time in the summer and winter, but even then there was no guarantee that they would attend school. Distance, poor road conditions, or brutally cold weather could conspire to keep them at home. So, too, could the costs of education. Private schools and academies charged fees that the poor could rarely afford, though sponsorship by an affluent patron permitted some disadvantaged students to attend. Children from large families were less likely to receive regular schooling than those from smaller ones. Common (or elementary) schools that received public subsidies still charged some tuition, and such schools were more plentiful in villages and towns than in widely dispersed farming areas. Even where communities or individual families sought the services of a teacher, one might not be available, and, given religious and moral sensibilities, available teachers might not be acceptable.

Given these obstacles, formal schooling, even where it was desired, was difficult to establish and sustain. Religious and social-class tensions also limited the prospects of forging social consensus around educational initiatives. Still, through a combination of actions taken by religious organizations, private citizens, and government authorities, an eclectic, if limited, form of schooling emerged in the early nineteenth century.

In the fishing colony of Newfoundland, a small number of schools were run by agencies working under the auspices of the Anglican, Catholic, and Methodist churches. The most significant among them was the Newfoundland

School Society, formed in 1823. Its teachers, mostly Anglican immigrants from England, worked throughout the
colony, including in areas where non-Anglicans lived. By
1831, it provided basic biblical instruction to more than
5,000 students in day schools or Sunday schools. The Education Act of 1836 authorized state funding to school districts
for the non-denominational elementary schooling of children from fishing families. But as historian Phillip McCann
notes, 'politico-religious disputes and faction fighting'
made broad agreement around this mission impossible to
achieve. Protestants, particularly from merchant and arti-
san families, had better educational opportunities than did
Catholics. The estimated level of literacy, especially among
fishers, was low. In 1843, public funds were divided between
Protestants and Catholics in a denominationally based system that would remain intact until the end of the twentieth
century.

In New Brunswick, the Parish School Act of 1802 provided some funding for common schools, though educational development was stifled by conflicts between Loyalist
Protestants and immigrant (largely Irish) Catholics, whose
numbers increased substantially after 1814. With the elected provincial Assembly now asserting greater influence,
schooling provisions improved. By 1845 some 500 schools
served 16,000 students. Facilities, however, were generally
poor, and teacher training was limited.

In Nova Scotia, denominational divisions also hampered
school development, and, by 1826, only 5,550 students were
enrolled in 217 schools. An important initiative, reflecting
growing interest in schooling, was taken in that year. Provincial legislation made it compulsory for each school district to establish a school if two-thirds of the district's
taxpayers requested one. (This was changed to a bare majority in 1836). The formal school system remained under-
developed, especially at the primary level, but school
promoters could point optimistically to other developments. Nova Scotia was the home of three colleges and

several academies by the 1830s, and of a lively cultural life featuring subscription libraries, newspapers, and scientific societies. As in Scotland, from which much of the Nova Scotian population originated, there were efforts to make education more accessible to ordinary citizens, though the ability to do so was by no means uniformly available. One of the first 'mechanics' institutes' in British North America was founded in Halifax in 1831, and over the next several decades these 'adult education' facilities appeared throughout the colonies. Initiated generally by 'influential citizens,' mechanics institutes were designed to contribute to the 'moral improvement' of workers by exposing them to scholarly lectures in the arts and sciences. That Nova Scotia had a secular and denominational common-school system spoke both to the popular interest in education and to the continuing conflict inspired by educational debates. In subsequent years, reform politicians such as Joseph Howe would take up the cause of public schooling, leading, as elsewhere, to the deeper involvement of the state in educational matters.

Prince Edward Island adopted a common-school act in 1825, providing for a combination of government and local funding of district schools. But conflicts between absentee landlords, who had little interest in supporting education, and tenant farmers, who pursued the cause, delayed educational development on the Island. Until the passage of the Free Education Act in 1852, the Island, like other Canadian colonies, relied on a combination of private, denominational, and partial state support for the provision of formal schooling.

Historians of Upper Canada have studied in considerable detail how this combination of formal and informal schooling evolved in the early nineteenth century. The research suggests that selective initiatives by the state combined with those of the 'voluntary' or 'discretionary' sector – family groupings, educational entrepreneurs, and religious crusaders – to produce a relatively high level of literacy in the province. The 1807 District School Act supported the establishment of a grammar school in each of the province's eight districts (later reconfigured as 'counties'). In 1816, the Common School Act, reflecting the fear of American influence in the colony following the War of 1812, required all teachers to be British subjects and to take an oath of allegiance to the Crown. Grants were provided for the establishment of common schools, but tuition remained in place, and teachers' salaries were appallingly low. By the mid-1820s, only 7,000 students were officially registered in common schools, and only 300 (all boys) in grammar schools.

However, additional classes were conducted in 'non-aided' schools, which depended entirely on private funding, and, as R.D. Gidney notes, between 1816 and the 1840s they were as numerous as those receiving government support. In 1849, while 738 students were enrolled in Kingston's common schools, 826 attended school programs held in other venues. 'Dame' schools, generally owned and operated by widows, appealed to families who wanted their daughters to obtain literacy, domestic skills, and appropriate cultural breeding. One such school in the 1830s was run by a Mrs Cockburn, who taught forty students from 'the best families in York [Toronto].'

Drawing students from a broader range of backgrounds, 350 to 400 Sunday schools, founded and funded by Christian churches, were teaching some 10,000 students in 1832. Frequently located in outlying locales, these schools were often the single outlets for children to obtain religious training and basic literacy.

Risk-taking teacher–entrepreneurs also established 'private venture' schools in the hope of securing contracts from parents for the instruction of their children. Schooling within private households, conducted by tutors, governesses, or parents themselves, was not unusual. James Durand, Sr, Esq. of Dundas advertised for 'a person thoroughly qualified to teach a young gentleman in various branches of education,' while Mary O'Brien resolved to teach her own children and another older girl. The latter would receive instruction in exchange for household service and child care. A group of parents in Norfolk County in 1826 drew up a contract with a teacher who would be able to teach children 'to read the word of God and transact their own business.'

Finally, academies, seminaries, and colleges, some of which received partial state funding, most of which did not, attracted children from middle-class families seeking something beyond 'common' school training. Grantham Academy of St Catharines was a coeducational school founded in 1829, while Upper Canada College, established in the same year, catered only to boys. Discouraged from attending (though not excluded from) state-supported grammar schools, women seeking advanced training often found better prospects in private academies. By 1840 there were twelve such institutions in the province.

Women who attended female academies in Upper Canada and elsewhere in the colonies would study the 'ornamental' subjects, also known as the 'accomplishments,' including drawing, painting, dancing, and modern languages. 'Careers' were highly unusual for female graduates, but their education was considered useful in the promulgation of middle-class virtues such as civility, sociability, and service to the church. Established in 1831, the Cobourg Ladies Academy set out to teach its students 'all the branches of education necessary to fit them for useful and elegant life.'

The development of schooling in Lower Canada from 1800 to the 1840s was similarly shaped by a mix of private, public, and religious forces, and by particular ethnic and linguistic tensions flowing from the Conquest. Dependent upon initiatives taken by the Catholic Church, which placed less emphasis on schooling than did Protestant evangelicals, educational opportunities for French Canadians were limited. At the turn of the century, the province's three major urban centres, with a combined population of about 33,000, had some eighteen elementary schools, eleven for boys and seven for girls. The rural population, totalling 128,000, was serviced by no more than thirty schools, fifteen each for males and females, the latter of which were run by a female religious order, the Congrégation de Notre-Dame. By contrast, the English-speaking Protestant population of Quebec, some 10,000 strong, had, by 1790, eighteen privately supported schools.

The Education Act of 1801, designed to expand state-administered schooling, permitted local parishes or townships to create schools and receive limited state funding for their maintenance. But the Royal Institute for the Advancement of Learning, which oversaw the system, was controlled by Protestants, and thus elicited little enthusiasm among Catholic leaders. Furthermore, the Catholic Church feared both the secularization of schooling under the authority of the state and the use of schools as instruments of assimilation into a Protestant, English-speaking culture. The Anglican bishop of Quebec, and a founder of the Royal Institute, Jacob Mountain, heightened francophone anxieties by calling for the 'Protestantization' of the Catholic population. In practice, the few 'Royal' schools created in French-speaking areas maintained their Catholic identities, but the system served English Protestant needs far more effectively. By 1829, eighty-four Royal schools were functioning, the majority of which enrolled English-speaking youth. McGill College, chartered in 1821, was established under the authority of the Royal Institute and stands as perhaps its most significant legacy.

The educational interests of French-speaking families were better addressed through the Syndics Act of 1829, a regulation which permitted locally elected trustees (or syndics) to administer the establishment of government-aided schools. Leading Catholic clergymen opposed this system as well because it threatened the authority of parish priests, whose involvement in new schools was not required under the act. Despite the rebuke of the Church, the

Syndics Act produced unprecedented results: the number of schools in the province quadrupled, to 1,282, between 1828 and 1832, as an estimated one-third of Lower-Canadian children were now exposed to some formal schooling. Andrée Dufour shows that, where education was available and affordable on the Island of Montreal, francophone school-attendance rates increased. That citizens themselves, more than Church officials, had supported the Syndics Act reflected the importance of community involvement in educational matters, a recurring theme in the life of the British North American colonies.

Secondary schooling in Lower Canada was provided to French Canadians in classical colleges, where males, largely from privileged families, would receive training primarily for the priesthood or the legal profession. By the 1830s, there were five such colleges and four seminaries. Large numbers of their graduates, however, were unable to find work in the province. Prestigious employment opportunities in business, public administration, and the military were taken up by anglophones, and there were insufficient positions in the liberal professions to meet the demands of classical-college graduates. Facing such frustration, many of them joined the 1837–8 rebellion against British rule.

Indeed, intensifying political conflict between the popularly elected Legislative Assembly and the non-elected Executive Council completely disrupted the educational system. School legislation was suspended in 1836, as was government financial assistance. Many schools closed, enrolments dropped, illiteracy persisted, and the colony was gripped by the outbreak and consequences of the rebellion.

For the first half of the nineteenth century, the western region of British North America, which included the area west of Upper Canada, was also preoccupied with priorities other than formal schooling. Through its chartered commercial agent, the Hudson's Bay Company, the British Crown sought to pursue its economic interests and assert its political authority over this vast territory. Native Indians and Métis (part Indian/part white), who comprised the vast majority of the population, were induced to participate in the fur trade, dominated until the 1860s by the Hudson's Bay Company. English- and French-speaking missionaries accompanied Hudson's Bay personnel to the region, intending to oversee the moral and educational tutelage of their children. Young people, however, often found the fur trade more alluring than the classroom, and their time in school was thus limited. Still, an organized religious presence enhanced the company's image, and it supported a number of educational initiatives. The first school at the Red River settlement opened in 1815; in the 1830s, a seminary for boys (which became the Red River Academy), and a girls' school, for the cultivation of the settlement's daughters, were established. By 1849, twelve schools served a Red River population of 5,391.

Typically, schooling in the early nineteenth century was conducted in private homes, churches, or primitive buildings that were not especially conducive to effective learning. Log 'shanties,' reinforced with moss and covered over with clay, were heated by open chimneys, which, in the absence of bricks, were assembled with clay and sticks. Damaging fires were frequent. Students of various ages worked on slates, and sat on benches placed along the length of the walls. Teachers were responsible for stoking the fires and cleaning the schoolroom.

'Itinerant' teachers, those who took up a position for a short time before moving on, probably to other teaching jobs, struggled for respectability in this period. Not only was their income minimal and intermittent, but their qualifications and living styles were frequently questioned. One writer described them as 'old men who had a mere smattering of learning and who were very incompetent instructors.'

Some, indeed, were barely literate and had little of value to offer students. But this was by no means universally the case. Teachers from the United States, where schooling opportunities were greater, were probably better educated than native-born Canadians. Financial need, more than lack of commitment, turned many of them into jobseeking transients – a common occupational pattern at the time. Poverty, more than sloth, compelled some to live in unenviable conditions, including sleeping in the schoolroom. Teachers who boarded with families often were active in the life of the community. While some educational entrepreneurs were more interested in earning dollars than in training scholars, others operated schools that set high standards and won the acclaim of their communities.

At the top of the teaching hierarchy were the male headmasters of grammar schools, who earned respectable incomes and had considerable prestige in their communities. Other teachers, including itinerant instructors in common schools, struggled to earn a living wage. Female teachers, whose numbers increased as the century progressed, were compensated poorly and had the least status. Typically, the New Brunswick School Act of 1833 authorized school trustees to pay women teachers no more than twenty pounds per year – half the salary received by their male counterparts. In the most indigent communities, teachers might be paid in kind – with flour and sheep, for example – not in cash. Those teaching in private academies that were supported by Church funds, or that could attract a loyal and continuous following of fee-paying students, fared better. That so many such institutions came and went in the first half of the nineteenth century signified the insecurity and temporality of the teaching vocation.

A popular teaching method before the 1830s, especially in the Maritimes and Quebec, was the monitorial system, promoted successfully by the British educators Joseph Lancaster and Andrew Bell. Both Protestant and Catholic school authorities favoured this form of pedagogy in larger schools because it was practical and cost-efficient. Through it, teachers would instruct those deemed the brightest students in the class, who would then be assigned the responsibility of teaching other groups of children. Student monitors would also take attendance, attempt to keep discipline, and serve other caretaking functions. The system was employed less in Upper Canada, where it was associated with the Anglican Church and thus viewed by others with suspicion.

Common-school teaching focused on instruction in basic or 'common' English education, unlike 'superior' schools, which included grammar schools, private academies, and classical colleges where students learned Latin and Greek. By most accounts, teachers stressed discipline, religion, recitation, and memory work. The 1831 'Rules for the Establishment of Schools in Lower Canada' required students to love God, defer to the master, be silent throughout class, clean the classroom, avoid idleness, and 'wash their hands and faces, also their feet if they are bare.' In addition, the children were to 'learn to spell words one syllable at a time,' and to write, using fingers or pointers, in sand instead of with ink on paper.

One alumnus of Cocagne Academy, a reputable school in Cape Breton, Nova Scotia, recalled the 'fear and truancy' it provoked among students 'rather than an enthusiastic thirst for knowledge.' The principal, a clergyman, taught ancient languages and history. 'But we learnt little more than lists of events and names of rulers. Of the life of the Greek people, of the effects of Roman institutions upon modern nations, and everything in fact that would be really useful for us to know, we remained ignorant.' Driven from class by 'brutal' discipline, truant students were also lured outdoors by the attractions of fishing, sugar making, and strawberry picking.

While inside the typical classroom, pupils partook in spelling bees and other forms of rote learning. The most impressive – and feared – of these was the annual public examination, in which students would be quizzed in front of family, friends, and even strangers from the surrounding community. In 1807, John Strachan invited 'all the respectable people within thirty miles' to witness the annual examination at his Cornwall school. Both the student's and the teacher's reputations could be affected by the published results of these memory-probing, character-building ordeals. The pedagogy reflected the importance schools assigned to cultivating the student's oral as opposed to written abilities. Instruction in good manners, good morals, and good taste comprised the 'hidden' curriculum of the colonial school, but in view of spare facilities, intermittent student attendance, and their own limited training, teachers could no by no means guarantee positive results.

While advanced education provided women and men with different experiences and opportunities, there were fewer gender-based distinctions evident in the curricula of common or elementary schools. Teachers concentrated on providing students with basic literacy, using the Bible as a primary text. Historians Susan Houston and Alison Prentice found that male students at the York (Toronto) Central School were being taught English, reading, writing, grammar, arithmetic, bookkeeping, and elements of geography, while girls were offered reading, writing, arithmetic, and drawing.

Education in the early nineteenth century was thus shaped by the forces of loyalism, Christianity, voluntarism, gender, and social class. State support was a modest stimulus to the extension of schooling, while the family's obligation to provide for its members' material needs kept many children at home, diminishing their opportunities for formal learning. Competing religious convictions both accounted for educational initiatives and stood in the way of cooperative schooling ventures. Instruction was provided in a variety of venues, the dominant form being common schools, which offered basic education. Advanced schooling for boys, available in grammar schools, private academies, or seminaries, stressed the importance of Greek and Latin, the knowledge of which enhanced one's social respectability. 'Superior' education for girls, furnished mainly in privately supported institutions, included academic, religious, and 'ornamental' studies designed to provide middle-class youth with a veneer of culture and refinement. By later standards, education hardly prospered in the British colonies between 1800 and 1840. By the standards of the day, school development was somewhat more impressive.

2

Building the Educational State

Educational change enveloped British North America from the 1840s to the 1870s. In a world being remade by extraordinary economic, technological, and political developments, schooling assumed new importance in the lives of both educators and ordinary citizens. Governments devoted unprecedented resources to the building, regulating, and sustaining of schools, and coercive – but largely popular – legislation empowered public authorities to pursue their educational goals. This chapter examines the background to and introduction of these significant initiatives.

In the 1840s, the Canadian colonies were in a state of flux. Upper and Lower Canada were recovering from political uprisings in 1837 and 1838 directed against what rebels had denounced as arbitrary rule by non-elected authorities. In each of the provinces, traditional 'tories,' impatient 'reformers,' and an assortment of other politicians who fit comfortably into neither camp wrestled with the problem of who should govern and by what means. Insisting on the virtues of 'responsible' government, which would enhance the power of elected politicians, an emerging class of businessmen, affluent farmers, lawyers, and other professionals rose to political and social prominence, played leading roles in the economic and cultural lives of their communities, and eventually led four of the original colonies – Nova Scotia, New Brunswick, Quebec, and Ontario – to Confederation in 1867.

For these officials, as well as for their critics, there were good reasons to support the expansion of public education. Prominent 'rebels,' such as William Lyon Mackenzie in Upper Canada and Louis-Joseph Papineau of Lower Canada, saw extended schooling as an important instrument of democratization. No longer should political authority or the opportunity for formal learning be the prerogative of the privileged. Ordinary citizens had the right to be educated and enlightened, and, as Mackenzie argued, society's élites in Church and government had no moral justification for continuing to 'keep [the people] in darkness.' Indeed, an educated populace would be better able to act in its own political interests.

For somewhat different reasons, the colonial politicians who exercised power during the 1840s, and who abhorred the rebels' radical politics, also came to understand the virtues of public education. For them the rebellions were a sign of a society in danger – threatened, without rule of law, by social collapse. Economic progress required civil order, and schools had a key role to play in ensuring political stability in a period of profound social change. Schools should cultivate the students' sense of citizenship, loyalty, respect for property, and deference to authority. As Egerton Ryerson, the superintendent of Ontario schools for some three decades, argued, education should prepare youth for their 'appropriate duties and employments of life, as Christians, as persons of business, and also as members of the civil community in which they live.' Only a system of public schooling, preferably free and compulsory, could effectively tackle such an important challenge. Unguided individualism – of students and teachers – posed great social risks, as the rebellions had proven.

Of equal concern was the example of the American Revolution and the type of society it had spawned. Canadian colonists in the mid-nineteenth century had mixed views of their neighbour to the south. Some political reformers, including descendants of Loyalist immigrants, were inspired by the democratic dynamics of American politics, the persistence of slavery notwithstanding. Many Canadians, too, were in awe of the rising economic power and prosperity of the United States, and aspired to similar standards of living in their own communities. The strides that Americans had made in public education were also admired by some noted Canadian schoolmasters and deemed worthy of emulation. But the majority of British North Americans were also certain of this: they did not want to be citizens of the United States.

For all of America's assets, Canada's élites frequently pointed to the 'dangers' of its republican way of life. Having repudiated their British heritage in the revolution of 1776, Americans were perceived as too individualistic, materialistic, aggressive, and disorderly, further evidenced by the gruesome and prolonged Civil War of the early 1860s. By contrast, Canada's leaders, including its educators, portrayed their own country as more civil, peaceable, ordered, and respectful of tradition. Even as the colonies' ties to Britain were loosened in the years leading up to Confederation, the cultural and emotional attachment to the monarchy, and all that it represented, remained strong.

Here, too, schools had an important socializing role. The ever-present British flag, homilies to the Queen, non-American textbooks, and the promotion of Loyalist mythology were a normal part of classroom life in English Canada in the mid-nineteenth century. As historian Bruce Curtis argues, it was the influence of the American tradition of dissent that especially concerned Canadian educators. If political critics could be characterized as disloyal as well as disruptive, then they might be more effectively marginalized and less able to obstruct the growing authority of the

Canadian state, including its administration of public schooling.

The desire for 'progress' and the fear of its side-effects thus informed the attitudes of middle-class school promoters. Growth, indeed, was unmistakable. Between 1841 and 1871, the Canadian population more than doubled, from 1.6 million to 3.9 million, and the country faced new economic challenges. Subjected by England to the forces of 'free trade,' Canadian producers and shippers lost their protected niche within the Imperial trading system during the 1840s, and were forced to consider other economic strategies. Signalling the revolutionary impact of steam power, railways offered a possible route to prosperity – and debt. Building them running them, and transporting goods and passengers on them, stimulated the first wave of industrial development in Canada. As Michael Cross and Greg Kealey note, trains 'captured the public's imagination and symbolically linked progress, science and capitalism together in a Victorian trinity of seemingly God-given articles of faith.'

At the same time, the established Canadian industries of fishing and lumber in the Atlantic region, and farming and grain production in central Canada, experienced, as always, the cycles of boom and bust. The 1830s had proven especially difficult for the farmers of Quebec, whose agricultural practices remained deeply traditional. In search of new opportunities, aspiring farmers from Ontario and some enterprising immigrants from northern Europe moved west to break land in the new province of Manitoba. They were not the first to establish roots there, however. Native Indians and Métis, having witnessed the demise of the fur trade, now confronted white settlement, 'Canadian' mounted police, and the forces of 'progress.'

Agricultural life still occupied most Canadians at mid-century, but, by then, some small villages had grown into thriving towns, where commercial life flourished. Saint

John, Halifax, Montreal, Toronto, and Hamilton were among the leading centres. There and elsewhere, according to Graeme Wynn, 'growth was a universal ambition.' Even centres such as Cobourg, Canada West (Ontario), whose population was barely 1,000 in 1842, had a variety of business and cultural outlets, including fourteen general merchants; ten hotels and taverns; several churches; and a number of tailors, tanners, cabinet-makers, and bakers. It also had four or five common schools, a new college, and two ladies' academies. Education increasingly was a central feature of the emerging urban landscape and of modern community life.

So, too, was the problem of pre-industrial poverty. Seasonal work in the forests and farms, on the canals and railways, drove transient labourers into the towns in search of housing and means of support. Their rugged and often ragged presence offended the sensibilities of middle-class citizens. To judge from reports of local newspapers and government-sponsored investigations, the poor – and their children – were a threat to the community's civil, moral, and aesthetic order. According to one education official in Toronto, 'the idleness and dissipation of a large number of children, who now loiter about the public streets or frequent the haunts of vice, [were] creating the most painful emotions in every well regulated mind ...' That increasing numbers of the indigent in the late 1840s were immigrants from the British Isles, particularly Ireland, suggested that Anglo-Saxon stock was a necessary but insufficient component of the genetic formula for social respectability. Class position mattered too, and, quite simply, it was best not to be needy.

If one were, then public schooling had special significance. Social reformers implored the sceptical to appreciate the logic of educating the poor. If poverty was caused by idleness, idleness by ignorance, and ignorance by the lack of schooling, then surely the community as a whole would benefit from investing in the education of the under-classes. Their children would be taught discipline, respect for private property, the virtues of manners, and morality. Juvenile delinquency would thus be prevented, or at least controlled. The poor would be subjected to the influence of the middle class, leading, ideally, to a state of class 'harmony.' In short, as Susan Houston explains, the community would be considered safer in a world of mass education. In response to one critic who opposed paying for the education of 'all the brats in the neighborhood,' Ryerson replied that educating 'brats' was the very purpose of his free-school legislation. 'It is proposed to compel selfish rich men to do what they ought to do, but what they will not do voluntarily.'

Whatever the social advantages flowing from the education of the poor, middle-class citizens, who had long de-pended on the 'voluntary' sector to school their children, could also derive direct personal benefits from a tax-supported system. By the 1840s, several provinces had already introduced 'local options' through which residents of school districts could vote to fund elementary schooling from public revenues, thus eliminating tuition fees and other privately borne educational expenses. As Robert Gidney and Wyn Millar have found, middle-class parents in Ontario also sought, with eventual success, to extend this principle to the financing of grammar schools, which socially advantaged children were the most likely to attend. Between the 1840s and 1870s, the number of publicly funded grammar schools in Ontario grew from about 12 to 100. In securing such support, 'people of property and substance ... were creating a school system designed primarily not for other people's children, but their own.'

The schools' custodial role included the realms of religion and morality. As noted earlier, denominational competition was rife in Canada during the early nineteenth century. Not only were Catholics and Protestants at odds over theological precepts, but Protestantism itself had a variety of doctrinal strains. Church-administered schools and colleges were intended to reflect and preserve these distinctions.

But proponents of mass schooling, drawn from various denominations, argued that Christian values could be promoted through other means that might have the added benefit of reducing religious tensions in every community. 'Public' schools should draw from a general tax base, thereby freeing individual denominations from the burden of financing education directly. At the same time, basic Christian morality could be taught in virtually every Canadian school. If the nation's children were exposed to a common spiritual message, then the moral foundation of the country could well be buttressed in a period of uncertain social change. Controversial clerical creeds were to have no place in public-school classrooms, but scriptural readings, the Lord's Prayer, and the Ten Commandments were both acceptable and required. Included in a New Brunswick school act of 1858 was the obligation of teachers to 'impress on the minds of the children ... the principles of Christianity, morality and justice ...,' a prescription echoed in other provinces.

The desire for non-denominational, broadly Christian schooling thus fuelled the campaign for public education, but total unity around religious matters remained elusive and, in most jurisdictions, unrealized. Catholic educators, both English and French, opposed the secular state's growing authority over education, nor did they believe that general Christian teachings sufficiently met their denominational needs. Catholic bishops from Ontario and Quebec released a statement in 1854 recommending the instruction of Catholic youth in 'orthodox doctrine,' funded on an 'equal footing' with the type of education provided in publicly funded schools. The zealous 'no popery' campaigns conducted in the 1850s by certain Protestant politicians, including some proponents of public schooling, deepened denominational rifts. Constituting a strong minority presence in English Canada, as well as the overwhelming majority in Quebec, Catholics secured a variety of arrangements protecting their denominational schools in several provinces, even during this period of educational expansion. So, too, did the Protestant minority in Quebec.

Indeed, this issue was critical to the nation-creating act of Confederation in 1867. The British North America Act (section 93) assigned to provinces the legislative and administrative responsibility for schooling. But so concerned were religious minorities that their legal rights to a religious educational would be withdrawn by intolerant provincial governments that the constitution guaranteed them. Where denominational schools existed in law at the time of a province's entry into Confederation, they would endure, and the federal government had the power to restore a denomination's educational privileges if they were threatened by provincial initiatives.

Consequently, separate (Catholic) schools persisted in Ontario. While all schooling was officially non-sectarian in the three Maritime provinces, following considerable debate and conflict, arrangements were made during the 1870s to preserve religious instruction in Nova Scotia and New Brunswick on the basis of local community initiatives. The issue of religious schooling had proven politically divisive in Prince Edward Island, but the Public School Act of 1877 entrenched the province's non-sectarian school system. Manitoba entered Confederation in 1870 with a dual school system of denominational (Protestant and Catholic) schools, while British Columbia joined Canada one year later committed to a completely non-sectarian process of public schooling. At the other end of the spectrum were Quebec and Newfoundland. The state played only a modest role in administering schools in both jurisdictions. Provincial funding instead was divided among Catholic and Protestant church authorities, who, subject to certain guidelines, governed their respective schools. In the absence of a non-sectarian school system, this created some tension-inducing anomalies as the population became more diverse. Quebec Jews, for example, were compelled to send their children to 'Protestant' or 'Catholic' schools.

All of this suggests that the campaigns for school expansion were 'top-down' projects, with social and religious élites controlling the agendas and determining the process of educational change. Their role was unmistakably central, but ordinary citizens had their own reasons for favouring the development of state-supported schooling.

It should be remembered that, at mid-century, the vast majority of Canadians lived in rural communities. They were aware of, but not yet consumed by, the forces of industrial and urban change. Schooling, however, could well play a role in their plans for the future. Farmers typically hoped their children, especially their sons, would eventually take over the homestead and preserve a rural way of life. But, in large families, there was not enough farmland to ensure the economic viability of everyone in the next generation, and alternatives had to be considered. In Ontario undeveloped rural sections were in short supply by the 1860s, and farm acreage was falling into fewer and fewer hands, adding to uncertainty about children's employment prospects.

Based on his examination of family wills, historian Chad Gaffield has hypothezised that parents 'came to consider sending their children to school as a means of giving to them a part of their inheritance.' In the distribution of family assets, allowance would frequently be made for the education of one or more children. It was hoped that such training would provide young people with the ability to secure 'economic competency' through other occupational pursuits. If schools were built in rural communities, children could prepare for the future without moving long distances from home. Even for those planning to remain on the farm, knowledge of accounting and the basics of mechanization would be useful in the world of commercial agriculture. According to this interpretation, given their practical concerns, many farmers were thus predisposed to the campaign for public education. Even without the propaganda from prominent school promoters, they could see the value of state-supported schooling.

A unique illustration of this attitude was evident in the campaign for free schooling in Prince Edward Island. From the founding of the settlement in the eighteenth century, a major source of conflict endured between absentee land- lords who owned large tracts of Island property, and the local population who worked the land as tenant farmers. The terms of 'employment' were dictated by complicated contracts drawn up between owners and tenants. Thus, the farming family's livelihood, legal rights, and economic prospects could well depend on the content of these intri- cate documents, prepared by local lawyers who were fre- quently considered to be biased in favour of the absentee owners. Literate farmers able to read and understand the contracts had distinct advantages over their illiterate coun- terparts, who were more exposed to exploitation and pov- erty. In light of this 'competence gap,' local residents called for publicly funded schools which, by ensuring basic lit- eracy, would strengthen the bargaining power of tenant farmers and contribute to their economic security. As Ian Ross Robertson notes, public education was 'a necessary means of self-help, and at the core of the Island's age of reform.' Indeed, in 1852, Prince Edward Island became the first jurisdiction in the British Empire to require province- wide free common schooling.

If political, religious, social, and economic conditions were grounds for extending schooling in Canada, so, too, were prevailing perceptions of the nature of childhood. Recent scholarship has challenged Philippe Ariès's influen- tial thesis that, from the Middle Ages through to the eigh- teenth century, there was no essential distinction between the ways children and adults behaved or were treated. In pre-industrial times children were indeed expected to work at very young ages, possibly at seven or eight, but childhood still had its own characteristics, defined, as Joy Parr notes, by 'youth cultures, apprenticeship bonds, childhood devotions, and law ...' Some historians have also claimed that, because they were perceived as 'little adults' until the eighteenth century, children were sexually and physically abused in their families and communities. There were indeed instances of this, but, as Linda Pollock's study of New England life in the sixteenth and seventeenth centuries has shown, most parents cared for their children, often in trying circumstances. Even in the Middle Ages, argues historian Shulamith Shahar, childhood 'existed' and 'parents invested both material and emotional resources in their offspring.'

In the nineteenth century, a variety of theories in Europe and North America attempted to explain the essence of childhood. Naturalists, drawing from the writings of the French philosopher Jean-Jacques Rousseau, portrayed children as innocents, budding flowers who required nurturing and cultivation rather than repression or restraint if they were to blossom into effective adults – a philosophy that would later influence 'child-centred' theories of education. More influential, however, were Christian theologians, who believed that children were possessed of original sin, constantly in danger of succumbing to moral temptations, and thus in need of continuous discipline. While less extreme in their views, most educators shared the belief that children were too untamed, unreasoning, or malleable to be left to their own devices. In the complex modern world, adults must regulate the child's environment, and schools were an increasingly important instrument of their socialization. The primary responsibility for child rearing was still situated in the private world of the family, but working parents, especially in urban areas, were not always able to supervise the daily activities of their children. Public schools could carry out this role, lending greater legitimacy to their growing custodial function.

So, too, schools could formalize and reinforce the process of socializing children according to prescribed gender roles. The sexual precociousness of young people was feared by most educators, and these anxieties increased as the children got older. From this perspective, restraining the passions of youth required keeping boys and girls apart; in most common schools in the 1870s, they sat in separate sections and, wherever practical, they were taught in different rooms. While both genders were normally taught from the same common-school curriculum, this was not the case at the secondary-school level. 'There was a very considerable diversity between the mind of a girl and that of a boy,' declared George Paxton Young, an Ontario grammar-school inspector in the 1860s, and, as we shall see, the system his department attempted to fashion was designed with this presumption in mind.

A mix of circumstances and motivations, then, accounted for the growing enthusiasm for public schooling. That school promoters in the mid-nineteenth century were not engaged in mere idle musing was evidenced by the enormous increase in actual school enrolments. Between 1841 and 1871, the number of students registered in 'publicly controlled day schools' rose fivefold, from 160,000 to 800,000. These figures by no means tell the whole story. They do not speak to the problem of irregular, let alone non-attendance (which the next chapter addresses), but they do reflect a major social transformation in Canadian society. Mass schooling – but something well short of universal education – had arrived.

It is important to note that Canadian families were inclined to send their children to school even before provincial laws compelled them to do so. Ontario was the first province, in 1871, to legislate compulsory attendance. Children between the ages of seven and twelve were required to attend school no fewer than four months per year. Prince Edward Island's first compulsory-school law was passed in

1877, Nova Scotia's in 1882, and New Brunswick's in 1905. British Columbia's mandatory-schooling legislation of 1901 was strengthened in 1921 to include children aged seven to fifteen. By 1916, eight provinces had compulsory-school laws. Quebec and Newfoundland avoided such legislation until 1942. Opponents of obligatory schooling in Quebec had long contended that such a law was unnecessary since students, increasingly, were attending school voluntarily, or at least on the orders of their parents. By 1900, according to the national census, Quebec had the country's highest rate of average daily attendance proportional to students enrolled.

Compulsory-school legislation, then, tended to follow, not precede, large-scale participation in public schooling. A more significant stimulus to school expansion was the availability of public funding. Where tuition fees and teachers' salaries were covered by revenues from taxation, enrolments rose. It is not surprising, then, that legislation providing such support was increasingly common in the period of rapid growth between 1840 and 1870.

Even prior to that era, the practice of allowing for free common schooling on the basis of the 'local option' was widespread. Where a majority of residents within a school district voted for property taxes, they could use the revenue to eliminate tuition fees and subsidize teachers' incomes. But, in the early nineteenth century, relatively few communities were able to afford to fund the schools they required. From the 1840s on, as economic growth, immigration, and settlement proceeded, local resource bases widened and the pace of school expansion increased. Interest in schooling deepened, and centrally administered free-school legislation acknowledged this reality.

Prince Edward Island's initiative in 1852 has already been noted. Nova Scotia passed a free-school act in 1865; Ontario, New Brunswick, and British Columbia in 1871; Manitoba in 1873. That 4,200 of 4,400 school sections in Ontario had voluntarily opted for free schools the year before the law made this practice compulsory reflected the extent to which support for state-financed education had already taken root.

Still the process leading to the public funding of elementary schooling had been far from smooth, and episodes of vigilant opposition to the cause merit attention. In Quebec, legislation was implemented in 1846 which required local taxation for the support of schools. This led to a violent uprising by disaffected *habitants* who, in 'la guerre des éteignoirs' (literally, 'the war of the candle-snuffers' accused of extinguishing the light of learning), burned down a number of schools, challenged the law by electing unqualified school commissioners, and refused to pay their taxes. They mistrusted the authority of the government and, at least initially, were unable to see how public schooling would serve their interests. The intervention of Jean-Baptiste Meilleur, the superintendent of education, and the Catholic clergy, which supported the law, helped quiet the controversy, and the virtues of publicly funded education, still under Church control, were eventually accepted. An 1849 amendment to the compulsory-funding law permitted a greater degree of local autonomy, but, by 1860, virtually all school districts in the province were funding their schools through taxation.

In Toronto, opposition to free-school legislation arose from economic, cultural, and political concerns. In 1847, the province had passed a law requiring cities and towns to finance schooling through local taxes. But the regulation provoked considerable opposition, in part because Toronto was enduring a depression at the time and new taxes were deemed intolerable. Equally potent was the complaint by Protestant Orangeman that public funds would pay for the education of Irish Catholic children whose families occupied a growing proportion of the city's population. 'Reform' politicians, who generally opposed the centralizing authority of government, also attacked the law for eroding municipal autonomy in the matter of school funding. The conflict led in 1848 to the closing of Toronto's schools for an entire year.

The controversy, however, soon passed, and, within two years, amid little opposition, the Toronto schools were supported by taxation and made tuition-free. An improved economy, new restrictions controlling the influx of Irish immigrants to the city, and amendments to the 1850 common-schools act designed to preserve local educational initiatives, including the election of school boards, diffused tensions.

British Columbians, as Jean Barman notes, lived through a period of uncertainty and change during the 1860s, fuelled by debate around free schools. Church-controlled (mainly Anglican and Catholic), fee-charging schools had, since the 1850s, provided the relatively few educational opportunities available in the two colonies of Vancouver Island and British Columbia. Exclusionary admission practices based on religion and social class elicited a movement for non-sectarian, tuition-free schooling, and in 1864 a law embracing these principles was passed. But in 1866, the same year that the two colonies amalgamated, a newly appointed governor, Frederick Seymour, declared his opposition to free schools. Reflecting the most conservative views of his privileged class, he argued that, without private tuition fees, even in public schools, society might be burdened with overly educated individuals who were not content with their appropriate place in the social order. 'Any man who respects himself would not desire to have his children instructed without some pecuniary sacrifice on his part.' Ultimately, however, these views were rejected, and British Columbia entrenched a free-school system in 1871, the same year that it entered Confederation.

The debates around state-regulated schooling point to an ongoing theme in the history of Canadian education: the tension between centralized, bureaucratic authority and local, community-based control. The laws governing financing and attendance included a multitude of other regulations affecting the election of school trustees, curriculum regulations, the inspection of classrooms, and the training and certification of teachers. The appointed officials who had authority over school systems, such as Egerton Ryerson in Ontario, Jean-Baptiste Meilleur in Quebec, and Alexander Forrester in Nova Scotia, favoured control from the centre, in which departmental officials would draw up educational regulations and oversee their implementation. As Ryerson wrote, 'To be a State system of Public Instruction, there must be a State control as well as a State law.'

This authority was exercised in a variety of ways. The 1846 Common School Act in Ontario empowered the provincial education office to standardize the use of school textbooks, and to classify them according to grade level. Previously, teachers used books on an *ad hoc* basis, with minimal accounting for their content, level of complexity, or place of origin. Consequently, American books, the most widely available, were in frequent use, which offended Ryerson and those who shared his Loyalist sensibilities. He denounced their 'anti-British and unpatriotic' messages and resolved to find an appropriate alternative.

This came in the form of the Irish National Readers, which were more politically reliable, denominationally non-controversial, and relatively cheap to purchase. Moreover, they were written for students at different academic levels, and thus were more suited to a graded school system. While American books did not immediately disappear from the schools, the move to a uniform curriculum, prescribed by education departments, took root in Ontario and elsewhere. New Brunswick introduced the Irish readers in 1846–7, and British Columbia did so as late as 1872.

Steps were also taken to formalize and standardize the certification of teachers throughout the colonies. In the early nineteenth century, there were few regulations governing the teaching applicant's scholarly credentials, though one's perceived moral character, nationality, and religion would be questioned and considered. As public schooling was extended, pressure mounted to 'elevate the tone' of school teaching and enhance its occupational credibility. Provincial education officials contended that consistent certification rules were required to achieve these ends. One indication of this was the creation of 'normal schools' for teacher training, the first of which was established in Toronto in 1847, followed over the next decade by similar institutions in New Brunswick, Nova Scotia, Prince Edward Island, and Quebec. Originating in France in 1834, the 'école normale' stressed the virtue of following standardized teaching norms. Egerton Ryerson described a normal school as one 'in which the principles and practices of teaching according to rule are taught and exemplified.'

But aspiring teachers were not required to attend normal schools in order to qualify, and their suitability to teach was determined by other means. In Nova Scotia in the 1860s, for example, candidates would be examined by a provincial board in five subject areas. They would then be licensed with a certificate grade ranging from A to E, depending on how they had performed on the exam. Gradually, throughout the provinces, standards were raised, and incentives were provided, both to school districts and to individual teachers to improve educational credentials. The more qualified the teacher, the more generous the school board's grant and the higher the teacher's salary.

School inspection was another facet of centralized authority which found expression in every provincial jurisdiction. Inspectors were expected both to collect information on the workings of individual schools and to ensure compliance with provincial standards. School inspection was a common feature of European and American school systems by the mid-nineteenth century, and leading Canadian educators were both aware of and influenced by these international precedents. Canadian inspectors – drawn from the more educated and privileged ranks of society – were intended to contribute to the efficiency of state-run institutions and, as Bruce Curtis contends, to cultivate among the population a 'civic morality,' rooted in middle-class values. Like the governments they represented, inspectors faced the challenge of acknowledging popular demands but controlling the excesses of democracy. A legislative committee in Quebec explained in 1853 that 'surveillance [of schools] ought to exist everywhere, and on the spot. This surveillance ought to be exercised by the Inspectors, conjointly with the local authorities ...'

By the 1870s, Canadian schools were more subject than ever to the authority of government legislators and regulators. As Ronald Manzer observes, cabinet ministers in the Maritimes 'were firmly in command of both educational politics and policy,' and in British Columbia, notes Thomas Fleming, the Department of Education had in place a system designed to 'control many aspects of school district operations, [including] the extent to which schools would be financed, the number of school boards that would exist, the organizational and administrative structures for the delivery of services, the character of the school curriculum, the nature of testing and standards, and criteria for teacher certification.'

But it would be a mistake to portray local officials – and the parents who lobbied them – as powerless in the matter of educational policy. All provincial school acts, like that in Ontario in 1846, permitted ratepayers to elect trustees to local school boards who were responsible for hiring and firing teachers and for maintaining school buildings. Teacher shortages frequently required school boards to recruit instructors with less than the minimum standard qualifications, and provincial school inspectors, acknowledging the dilemma, were known to turn a blind eye to this practice. At the same time parents who objected to the presence of incompetent teachers might keep their children at home, complain to local authorities, or confront the problem directly by verbally or, worse, physically assaulting the offending instructor. The parents' actions could, but did not invariably, produce the results they desired.

Given their ambitious plans, but limited personnel – educational bureaucracies were still staffed by very few people – provincial authorities required local cooperation to achieve their ends. Ronald Manzer contends that the dominant model of governance in the nineteenth century was 'provincial control of educational policy and local management of schools.' Ryerson's strategy of 'informing and advising local authorities, explaining their responsibilities, and arbitrating local disputes' was emulated by Quebec's Jean-Baptiste Meilleur, who believed in the practice of 'policy tutelage,' that is, central control with local compliance. The history of free-school legislation, as we have seen, illustrated this course of action. Provincial authorities everywhere understood that complete public funding was achievable only if taxpayers, in the context of their local communities, were prepared to support it. The complex, and at times tempestuous, relationship between the forces of centralism and localism infused the politics of education in the nineteenth century, and well into the twentieth.

The support for publicly funded and centrally administered elementary schooling took root gradually in the Canadian provinces, and the systems that emerged were by no means identical. Still, common influences, patterns of growth, and administrative strategies could be identified in the construction of state-run schooling. A pre-industrial society in transition, Canada confronted the challenges that change unleashed. While encouraging 'progress,' society's middle-class leaders sought ways of protecting themselves from its most unpalatable consequences, and schools were seen as instruments of both order and stability. Not only could educators occupy the time of students, but they could imbue them with attitudes designed to make society both productive and governable. Ordinary Canadians, however, did not really need to be dragged to the schoolhouse door, though the poorest among them found it difficult to attend regularly. They too hoped to reap the benefits of society's investment in public schools. Whether they would remained to be seen.

3

Teachers and Students

What went on in the Canadian classroom in the last half of the nineteenth century? Having secured legislative and popular support for publicly funded education, school promoters faced the challenge of delivering on their elaborate promises. If education were to facilitate orderly social change on a scale hitherto unforeseen, then provincial authorities had a number of pressing tasks. They had to recruit qualified teachers, increase the capacity of schools, keep students in the classroom, and prepare the curriculum. They had, in short, to meet grand expectations largely of their own making.

A native of Parrsboro, Nova Scotia, Annie Leake and her twelve siblings were the children of a farmer/carpenter who barely earned enough to support his family in the 1850s. With little more than a year of formal schooling, Annie left home at the age of ten to work as a servant in her uncle's household. Over the next several years, she combined domestic work with periodic schooling and, inspired by the desire for independence, the love of learning, and an evangelical conversion experience at the age of seventeen, she resolved to become a teacher. Short-term teaching provided her with enough money to attend the new normal

school in Truro, which then qualified her to teach anywhere in Nova Scotia. Periodically unemployed, she held
several positions over the next fifteen years, including one
at the Truro Model School, where she supervised student
teachers. Earlier she had worked in one-room schools
so poorly equipped that she was compelled to maintain
the buildings and provide her own teaching aids. Widely
respected for her skills – which included accolades from
Alexander Forrester, the province's superintendent of education – she frequently lamented the minimal income and
security that teaching provided. In 1876, she took a job in a
St John's model school, teaching up to a hundred students,
again for a meagre salary. As Marilyn Färdig Whiteley reports, she left Newfoundland and the teaching profession
ten years later, working ultimately in a rescue home for
prostitutes in Victoria, British Columbia.

Annie's fellow Nova Scotian James McGregor McCurdy
had attended the Pictou Academy, obtained a teaching
licence, but then moved to Moncton, New Brunswick, in
1854, where he operated a book and stationery store. Admired for his high-educational standing, McCurdy resumed
teaching and opened a 'Superior School,' offering a high-
school curriculum, including the subjects of mathematics
and the classics. By 1868 his highly reputed school had a
staff of four. Following the passage of the province's Common School Act in 1871, McCurdy entered the public-
school system, in which, as a leading community educator,
he taught until his death in 1886.

These two careers reveal much about the nature of teaching in the late nineteenth century. As the school system
expanded, it offered new vocational opportunities for ambitious young people from modest backgrounds. The continuing mobility of teachers reflected both the growing
interest in public schooling and the difficulty many communities still faced in providing adequate facilities. New 'normal' and 'model' schools pointed to provincial efforts to
improve teachers' qualifications. Whatever one's creden-

tials or experience, schoolteaching offered different career trajectories for men and women. Even though she took advanced courses at the Mount Allison Wesleyan Academy, Annie Leake was confined to teaching positions with low status and minimal salaries. James McCurdy, by contrast, found more security and prestige as a secondary-school teacher. Among Canadian educators, these were common experiences.

A good illustration of what educational authorities expected of schools and teachers was found in the planning and governing of 'normal' schools. These novel teacher-training institutions, which existed by 1860 in all Eastern provinces except Newfoundland, were designed to raise, beyond mere competence – or, in some cases, incompetence – the level of classroom instruction. If aspiring teachers themselves were subjected to a demanding, regulated, and standardized course of study, then their future students could reap the benefit of this experience. As Bruce Curtis notes, Normal School students ideally would acquire 'the habits, skills, and the character structure appropriate to the morally forceful teacher.'

This was to be accomplished through a rigorous academic program that occupied the student's entire weekday, and then some. Lectures were delivered Monday to Friday from 9:00 A.M. to 1:00 P.M., 2:00 P.M. to 4:00 P.M., and 6:00 P.M. to 8:00 P.M. and repetition classes were held on Saturday mornings. Like its counterpart in Saint John, New Brunswick, which covered nineteen subjects in twelve weeks, the Toronto school featured an extraordinarily heavy curriculum. This included the subjects of parsing (grammar); the art of reading; mathematical, physical, and political geography; linear drawing; history; geometry; algebra; trigonometry; physics; and agricultural chemistry. 'Miscellaneous' subjects – music, composition, orthography (spelling), and the philosophy of education – were taken outside regular classroom hours. Students also spent an hour a day at a model school, observing or engaged in practice teaching. Normal-school pedagogy, which stressed rote learning and memorization, was not universally acclaimed. The parent of one Ontario student complained that the student teachers were suffering 'mental and physical stress,' the result of being taught 'too much in too short a time.'

The normal school's behavioural code was similarly severe and extended beyond the classroom. Punctuality, compliance to authority, evening curfews, regular church attendance, and gender segregation were obligatory. Typically, the McGill Normal School in Montreal permitted no 'intercourse between male and female pupil-teachers while in school, or when going to, or returning from it.' Students periodically circumvented, or even resisted, such uncompromising regulations. An 1853 petition at the Toronto Normal School criticized the 'outrageous' and 'needless restrictions' on student life, but the agitators, threatened with suspension, apologized for their defiant behaviour. In 1863, three Toronto students were expelled for writing 'anonymous letters to members of the opposite sex.' Aspiring teachers may have endured such petty regulations because a normal school certificate enhanced their vocational prospects. Graduates could be hired anywhere in the province without having to sit for county examinations every time they applied for a new teaching position.

While a minority of Canadian teachers – only one-quarter in Ontario – had received such professional instruction by the 1870s, the general level of their educational backgrounds rose. Most elementary teachers, with or without normal-school credentials, had some high-school training, and secondary-school teachers increasingly were attending university. In a growing economy, with a variety of employment prospects – mainly for men – this was a significant development. If teacher qualifications were to improve in a period of expanding school enrolments, new recruitment strategies were required. How, in light of potential teaching shortages, did educators meet the demand for public schooling? The answer lay in the employment, in ever-larger numbers, of female teachers.

Applying this approach was, to some degree, an ideological and cultural challenge. Traditional Victorian values militated against the engagement of women in anything other than household work. The editor of *The Provincial*, a Nova Scotia magazine, asserted (in 1852) that a woman 'occupies the position which her Creator intended her to fill, that of "help meet [mate] to man."' Consequently, she should engage in no activity that might interfere with family or domestic responsibilities.

But more enlightened school promoters, eager to staff the classrooms, were able to justify the appointment of women on grounds that exploited rather than offended Victorian sensibilities. Alexander Forrester, Nova Scotia's superintendent of education, conceded that by the 'law of nature and revelation' women were 'subordinate' to, but also were kinder and more affectionate than, men. They were therefore well equipped to teach very young children, whereas male teachers were better suited to educating the more 'advanced' classes, and to schoolmasterships. By this logic, women could preserve their nurturing role and employ it in the service of the state without threatening the status of men. At the same time, given its connection to the practice of child rearing, teaching could serve as a training ground for young single women destined for marriage. Wrote one Nova Scotian school inspector, 'The family is the school in which the married lady should teach.' That women had already been visible as teachers in private academies and 'dame' schools, and had long provided Catholic education in Quebec and elsewhere, made their conspicuous presence in the public schools less of a novelty than it otherwise might have been.

By 1870, women comprised some 60 per cent of public-school teachers in Canada, and, by 1900, some 77 per cent. Clearly the expansion of the provincial school systems would have been impossible without their recruitment. That they were paid on average half as much as their male counterparts underscored the economic rationality of hiring them. In 1851, Jean-Baptiste Meilleur, Quebec's chief superintendent of education, explained that 'services [of women] can be had at rates which bear much more lightly on the rate payers.' While males (in the 1870s) earned annually between $250 and $400, women were paid $150 to $300. But public-school salaries, including those of women, compared favourably with those of other industrial workers, whose average annual wage in Ontario in 1871 was $252. As schooling expanded, labour-market shortages in some regions might well have worked to the economic advantage of teachers. On the other hand, there were reported cases, especially in very poor rural communities, of teachers, usually women, being paid next to nothing and forced to make do with board and lodging. Able to find alternative employment on farms, in the timber trade, on railways, or in industry, men were less subject to such penurious conditions. Secondary-school teachers earned much higher salaries than their elementary-school counterparts – some 65 per cent more in Ontario in 1882. Women secondary-school teachers, whose numbers gradually grew towards the end of the century, were paid far less than men in the same schools, but still more than male elementary-school teachers.

The 'feminization' of teaching, then, owed a great deal to the employment of thousands of women at relatively low wages. But, as a number of historians have discovered, the patterns of recruitment were not identical nationwide. By way of example, in 1881, four-fifths of Toronto public-school teachers were women, and their proportion increased in subsequent years. In Montreal, however, women lost ground, and by 1900 they were a minority in the schools run by the city's Roman Catholic School Commission. Female teachers in Quebec were instead concentrated in private and domestic education, particularly in convent schools, whose numbers increased significantly in the late nineteenth century. Whereas coeducation had become the norm in Ontario, segregated teaching was promoted with new vigour in Quebec's Catholic schools. In this sector, both the teaching of girls and the recruitment of female instructors were de-emphasized, as Catholic school boards secured higher provincial grants for employing male teachers.

At the same time, women were a significant presence in the rural districts of both provinces, but in the Quebec countryside, they were hired earlier in the century and remained a dominant force longer than their counterparts in 'frontier' Ontario. As Alison Prentice and Marta Danylewycz explain, in both provinces males were preferred and employed in rural areas where they were available; given the comparative patterns of immigration and economic growth, there were more rural men for hire in Ontario than in Quebec. Unable to support their families, Quebec farmers migrated by the thousands to the factories and mills of Montreal and New England. In western Canada, which had the country's highest proportion of male teachers, men outnumbered women in the population, compounding the problem of teacher shortages. As a result, men frequently combined the occupations of farming and teaching. Patrick Harrigan correctly notes that a full understanding of the 'feminization' of teaching requires more comparative research on the cultural life, demographic developments, and local economies of Canadian communities. Case-studies, such as those just described, allow for the following conclusion: women were hired in growing numbers to staff a costly and rapidly expanding school system because qualified male teachers were in short supply.

The challenges of staffing notwithstanding, school enrolments rose steadily in the last four decades of the nineteenth century. According to official statistics, some 600,000 students were registered in public schools in 1861 compared with 1.1 million in 1901, an increase of 83 per cent. Over the same period, the Canadian population grew from 3.2 million to 5.3 million, an increase of 65 per cent.

Taken alone, the enrolment figures obscure the problems of inaccurate counting, irregular attendance, and the disparity of school participation rates by region and social class. In 1880, an average of 58 per cent of students who were registered in public elementary and secondary schools across the country attended class on a regular basis, which in Ontario was interpreted as more than 100 of 244 school days per year. By 1900, only 61 per cent of Canadian youth age five to fifteen were consistent school attenders. Throughout the country, rural attendance rates lagged behind those in urban centres. As one local superintendent in Ontario had claimed in 1871, 'irregularity of attendance is the bane and curse of the public schools; it is a log and chain upon the progress of instruction for it blasts and withers the noblest purposes of the best of teachers.'

Universal school attendance, then, even during this era of expansion, had yet to be realized (though, as Robert Gidney and Wyn Millar point out, the school year in Ontario in the 1980s of some 185 days was far shorter than it had been a century earlier). Intermittent participation in schooling had several causes, including the practice of child labour. As we noted earlier, children had habitually worked on farms, and rural youth continued to do so in the last part of the century. Even as their parents acknowledged the importance of schooling and increasingly sought to make it available, the needs of the farm dictated the frequency and timing of school attendance. Labour-saving machinery made farm work somewhat less onerous for the family, but it did not offset the growing shortage of agricultural labour; farm hands, including those of children, were still at a premium.

Nor were city youth entirely freed from the burden of working life. Factory production, a technological novelty in the age of steam-driven power, found innovative ways to exploit working-class children as young as nine or ten. In the tobacco, textile, coal-mining, and other industries where small stature and nimble fingers could be profitably engaged, employers occupied school-age youth in non-educational activities. Historians have discovered that, in the wake of growing industrialization and the demand for labour, the percentage of boys over twelve attending school in Hamilton, Montreal, and Orillia was lower in 1871 than in 1861. In the early 1880s, children constituted an estimated 11 per cent of the Toronto workforce. Like compulsory-education legislation, laws prohibiting child labour were introduced in several provinces and, initially at least, minimally enforced. Nor did the law itself, even theoretically, always afford protection to young workers. An 1873 statute in Nova Scotia prohibited boys from working in mines until they were ten, and allowed their employment for up to sixty hours a week only when they reached age twelve. Working- class girls under sixteen were less likely than boys to find industrial work and, consequently, as in the case of the city of Hamilton, attended school more regularly. But owing to the demands of domestic service, in their own homes and those of others, such young women appeared at school less frequently than did their middle-class counterparts. While elementary schooling was tuition-free, the cost of books, supplies, even new shoes, proved burdensome for the most indigent, impeding their children's prospects for continuous tutelage. The participation in public schooling of all social classes increased in the late nineteenth century, but the children of the working poor showed up for class less often, and exited the system earlier, than those from better-endowed families.

The primitive conditions of many schools further frus-

trated the achievement of comprehensive and uninter-
rupted education. The best-equipped facilities were found
in prosperous urban communities with healthy tax bases.
Newly constructed elementary schools were organized by
grades, each conducted by different teachers with comparatively strong qualifications. Their classrooms would include
modern teaching aids such as blackboards, maps, and up-
to-date textbooks. Within the same city, however, were
other schools that were overcrowded, poorly ventilated, and
under-supplied. One observer described a beginners' class
at Borden Street School in Toronto this way: 'The little
things are packed so closely upon the benches that they
often have to sit with their shoulders fitting in towards the
back of the seat sideways.' Ontario's pupil/teacher ratio
stood at seventy-two to one in 1877, though it improved to
forty-nine to one by 1902. In Newfoundland, the Catholic
school inspector lamented the condition of his schools in
1871: 'buildings in disrepair, small attendance, few books,
poor teaching and low pupil ratio.'

One-room schoolhouses, where a single teacher taught
students of all ages and at various academic levels, characterized rural education throughout Canada well into
the twentieth century. Securing teachers, let alone well-
qualified ones, plagued educational authorities, compounding the problem of irregular student attendance. A
Prince Edward Island school inspector reported in 1882
that 10 per cent of the 160 schools he visited were closed,
even as new schoolhouses were being constructed elsewhere in the province to meet anticipated demand. In rural
Quebec in 1905, some 400 Protestant schools had an average attendance of about 10. Even where available, country
schools were not always accessible. Poor weather and ill
health, in addition to farm labour, could keep children
from trekking up to two miles a day to and from class. The
proliferation of rural schools with small enrolments led, as
we shall see later, to the controversial practice of school
consolidation.

Still, classroom crowding was by no means unknown in the countryside, reflecting both parents' enthusiasm for schooling and their frustration over inadequate facilities. Houston and Prentice describe a schoolhouse in Durham County, Ontario, which was built to seat 30 students. But, in 1869, 136 students showed up for registration, and 70 to 100 attended regularly. To cope, the teacher sent 15 to 20 children outdoors to play, leaving the remainder clustered inside for daily lessons. Fortunately a new building, seating up to 90 students, was erected the following year, more adequately meeting the demand.

Whether sparsely filled or uncomfortably cramped, the classroom was the principal citadel of public education. Subjected to departmental regulations, parental demands, and the chore of schooling students from diverse backgrounds with a range of abilities, teachers had a challenging task. The books they used and the pedagogy they practised reflected aspects of Canada's social and cultural life. What children were expected to learn, and how they were taught, signalled, in part, the dominant values of their communities.

Overwhelmingly Christian, the Canadian provinces, as we have seen, created schools with strong moral purposes. In the denominational systems of Newfoundland and Quebec, and in the separate schools of Ontario, explicit doctrinal teachings were promoted and endured. But Christian teachings were found in other jurisdictions too, where the challenge was to respect religious sensibilities without offending sectarian loyalties. Through the Canadian Series of School Books, used in the 1870s in British Columbia and elsewhere, children were taught that God not only created the universe, but was the source of kindness and intellect, and that to absorb his goodness, one should read the scriptures daily.

By the end of the century, however, as Harro Van Brummelen notes, religious messages were taught less literally in public schools, and adapted instead to the preoccupations of commercial life in a more secular, urban society. Teachers used Bible stories to buttress moral lessons, including the 'Golden Rule,' and to promote the virtues of a 'productive life.' Like biblical heroes, students were encouraged to 'work hard, use their time well, and to be humble, prudent and courageous.' According to Robert Bérard, Nova Scotia's teachers were advised to cultivate 'Christian morality' among students by teaching the virtues of honesty, loyalty, sobriety, frugality, and chastity.

Educators expected students in primary schools to learn how to read and write, but mere literacy begged the question of how students were being taught and how well they understood their lessons. Attaining social respectability required one to speak proper English, free of unrefined vernacular, and to be attentive to the principles of order and uniformity. By the 1870s, current pedagogy stressed the importance of expression; correct enunciation was rewarded, inelegant articulation deplored. Penmanship, too, was now being emphasized, with similar attention to style and standardization. Using goose-quill pens, students, according to one instruction manual, ought to 'write in unison so that they not only make the same letter but the same part of the letter at the same time.' Precise diction and polished script drawn from classical English texts impressed classroom observers but less adequately reflected the depth of students' real knowledge. As George Tomkins notes, the classroom focus on presentation 'confused oral performance with cognitive skill with the result that comprehension was often wrongly assumed to have been achieved.'

Cultivating an image of respectability was one instructional aim; another was preparing students for the 'daily pursuits of industrial and domestic life.' There was a limit, however, to the range of practical studies offered in schools before the turn of the century. Following Ontario's example in 1871, a number of provinces introduced courses on agriculture and basic bookkeeping. The latter was to aid males destined for commercial occupations, and to be used by women in the 'household economy.' Boys were offered cadet training as early as the 1860s, which, by the 1880s, had become the basis for physical-exercise and calisthenic programs. Proponents contended that these drills would encourage 'manliness,' thwart effeminacy, and produce 'muscular Christians' who would contribute to the moral regeneration of Canadian society. Girls, in the meantime, were taught to knit, sew, and weave, activities that were later formally incorporated into domestic-science courses.

In a period marked by the territorial expansion of the British Empire, English-Canadian educators sought to instil in schoolchildren a passionate commitment to their Anglo-Saxon heritage and identity. The 'Loyalist cult,' which was especially influential in Ontario, spread to other regions by the turn of the century. Empire Day in the schools, first celebrated in Nova Scotia and Ontario in 1899, coincided with Queen Victoria's birthday, and featured songs, displays, and parades commemorating the past and linking Canada's fate to that of Britain's.

In French-speaking Quebec, however, such rituals held little appeal. Regulated by the clergy, Catholic schools stressed religious instruction and the teaching of French over English. Like their Protestant English counterparts, these schools taught mathematics, geography, drawing, natural science, civics, and Canadian history. The gap between the cultures was especially evident, however, in the way history was interpreted in school texts. While English books concentrated on the experience of Britain and English Canada, and celebrated the bond between them, French publications, largely written by clerics, highlighted religious themes, the impact of the Conquest on Quebec, and the continuing struggles faced by the French-Canadian minority. Canadian history that did not bear on the Quebec experience was largely unexplored.

The pursuit of morality, patriotism, and utility, then, impelled elementary-school teaching in the late Victorian era. Sitting in large classes, students were directed en masse, in lock-step fashion, through a series of academic stages (grades or 'forms') designed both to strengthen their minds and gradually to fill them with mountains of culturally suitable information. The theory of 'mental discipline,' promoted throughout the country, conceived of the mind as a 'machine or muscle ... a tool to be sharpened, honed and polished by the application of certain kinds of subjects to it.' Knowledge was rigidly compartmentalized in a way that fit scientific notions of how one learned. According to the principles of 'faculty psychology,' the brain was divided into discrete sections, facilitating memory, reasoning, imagination, and morality. To avoid a distorted intellectual and social development, the student must be taught a precise quantity of reading, arithmetic, geography, and science in exactly the right order. In the view of New Brunswick's chief superintendent (1881), if classroom instruction was orderly, demanding, and balanced, then students would cultivate occupationally useful skills: earnestness, concentration, self-control, and self-development. The employment, too, of 'object teaching,' which sought to engage students with questions and demonstrations, rather than merely submitting them to lectures, was a mid-century innovation intended to enhance formal learning.

These, at least, were the objectives of classroom instruction. The reality frequently was less impressive. A former elementary student recalled the pervasiveness and drudgery of drills and memorization: 'The whole class would commit to memory facts, grammatical and arithmetical rules, etc. by repeating them in a sort of sing-song chant.' Students also learned history and geography by accumulating information in a rote-like manner, a process, according to Robert Stamp, which 'often killed any natural curiosity young minds might have had about these subjects.' Sometimes, the teacher's mission was even more basic. If she kept students in their seats and merely taught them how to read, then, in the opinion of one Nova Scotian observer, 'she would be safe from interferences on the part of parents and trustees.'

Teachers in the one-room school faced particular challenges, not only in holding students' attention, but in simultaneously teaching a variety of subjects to children of different ages. Effective instruction required organization, innovation, and luck. Historian Jean Cochrane describes the classroom atmosphere and the teaching techniques, which employed a version of the old monitorial system. 'When work started, even with the best of teachers in the best-behaved school, the room was full of noises and the distinct possibility of confusion, as children in eight grades were put through their paces. To get to everyone and every subject, the teacher's presentations were usually only a few minutes long, and while she worked with one small class the rest of the children did seat work and consulted with older, wiser people in grade four or six, whom they were allowed to ask for help.' Preparing grade-eight students for the high school–entrance examination was the most daunting academic test in the rural school; the child's future and the teacher's reputation could well depend on student success rates. Still, by 1920, fewer than one-fifth of rural students in Canada enrolled in high school. Even where their children excelled, families often could not afford to send them away to urban high schools.

In country and city schools alike, ensuring classroom order tested teachers' mettle in every era, and this was certainly true in the mid- to late nineteenth century. Having yet to secure assured professional standing in their communities, elementary-school teachers were especially vulnerable to challenge and provocations by students and their parents. Facing large classes and pervasive stereotypes regarding the 'frailty' of women, female instructors were most exposed to the problem of classroom disorder. To cope, teachers employed a variety of strategies, ranging from gentle persuasion to brute force. The birch rod, commonly used in the first half of the century, helped teachers apply the theory that 'punishment and fear of punishment' would most effectively break the will of the overly assertive child. Corporal punishment of this sort was subsequently viewed more critically by school authorities, and, by 1880, as C.E. Phillips notes, it was 'condemned in most educational literature' for its inhumanity and questionable effectiveness. Departmental regulations, such as those issued in New Brunswick in 1863, called for restraint, on the premise that student self-discipline and voluntary cooperation were the most productive instructional tools. Teachers were advised to 'exercise such discipline as would be pursued by a judicious parent in his family.'

But these guidelines were deliberately vague, and left the teacher with considerable discretion. Some used ridicule, reprimand, detentions, deprival of privileges, and suspension to control recalcitrant students. Others, in a more inventive spirit, opted for positive reinforcement over censure and repression. Befriending students and their families was a possible, if exceptional, technique for gaining authority and respect. New pedagogies, offering incentives and rewards, were increasingly common in the late-nineteenth-century classroom. As Houston and Prentice explain, 'merit cards' denoting 'punctuality, good conduct, diligence and perfect recitations' were assigned to the most outstanding students, who received book prizes for their exemplary efforts. Regulation and classroom order were also imposed through new technological innovations designed for large classes in multipurpose schools. The omnipresent school bell called students to class, immovable desks arranged in rows confined them there, and blackboards riveted their gaze to the front of the room.

Notwithstanding these alternative disciplinary techniques, corporal punishment endured. At Ottawa's Central School East, some sixty strappings a month were dispensed throughout the 1880s. Jesse Ketchum Public School in Toronto strapped two students a day over a two-week period in late 1888. Such rule violations as 'fighting, misbehaving in line, lying, eating in school, neglecting to correct wrong work, shooting peas in the classroom, going home when told to remain, long continued carelessness, and general bad conduct' could earn the Jesse Ketchum student between four and twelve beatings on the palm. In managing the classroom, fear and violence still had their uses, though teachers who habitually beat students and roused the ire of parents could find themselves driven out of the school and into court on charges of assault. In the emerging world of educational bureaucracy, discipline itself was subject to regulation, but the rules of enforcement were far from crystal clear.

Though not unknown, corporal punishment was applied less often in secondary schools, where students were older and expected, without the aid of the teacher's heavy hand, to maintain a high level of deportment and self-discipline. The development of what commonly became known as the 'high school,' with similar characteristics nationwide, has its roots in the late Victorian era, where the Ontario experience again proved influential.

As we noted earlier, 'superior' schooling in the first half of the nineteenth century comprised a mix of publicly subsidized grammar schools and academies run by Christian denominations or private entrepreneurs. Because they were more affordable, grammar schools grew in popularity among middle-class families, and by the 1860s had become Ontario's dominant form of post-elementary education. Egerton Ryerson, and his newly appointed secondary-school inspector, George Paxton Young, believed that grammar-school standards – especially the teaching of Latin and Greek – were uneven and required firmer direction from provincial authorities. In 1871, the Common

School Act created two secondary-school streams: collegiate
institutes, which taught the classics and were designed for
boys destined for university, and the coeducational,
workplace-oriented high schools, which concentrated on
English, commercial subjects, and natural science.

But as Robert Gidney and Wyn Millar's penetrating study
of the origins of Ontario secondary education demonstrates, organized citizens, through their local educational
districts, foiled Ryerson's plans for post-elementary schooling. During the 1860s, parents continued to send their
daughters to grammar schools, despite 'official' objections,
and they resisted provincial efforts to close down 'low-
quality' grammar schools for fear of losing complete access
to secondary education. Furthermore, they resented the
privileged status that would flow to collegiates, which, under the terms of the 1871 act, would be open only to a tiny
minority of the population. As a result of local pressures
and government compromises, the distinctions between
the collegiates and the high schools diminished, and a
common curriculum, available to males and females,
emerged. By the late 1870s, girls constituted nearly half of
the secondary-school enrolment, and, in the 1880s, the
typical core course of study consisted of English, history,
modern languages, science, the classics, and mathematics.
With the exception of additional classes in commercial
studies, which were vocationally oriented, the curriculum
was strongly academic and intended to refine the students'
'mental culture.'

In other regions of Canada, composite secondary schools
with a strong academic focus also emerged before the end
of the century. The high-school curriculum in the North-
West Territories (Alberta and Saskatchewan) drew from
textbooks that had been authorized for use in Ontario, and
was designed with teacher preparation in mind. As Bernal
Walker notes, 'English was enthroned as the king of the
subject-matter fields in territorial high schools.' Prose readings were drawn from the classics of English literature, such

as Shakespeare, and poems, typified by the work of Wordsworth and Tennyson, highlighted the Romantic and Victorian eras. Geography courses covered the world, but paid particular attention to the territory of the British Empire. Similarly, history classes concentrated almost exclusively on the study of Britain and Canada. As enrolments grew, the pressure to broaden the range of vocational subjects intensified, a common demand of urban school reformers throughout the country.

While not immune to such appeals, secondary schooling in Quebec followed a different route from that in English Canada. English-speaking students in that province attended high schools that resembled those elsewhere in the country, but, for Quebec francophones in the Catholic system, there were no high schools as such; classical colleges, of which there were nineteen in the province by the turn of the century, trained males destined for university and/or professional careers. Deeply bound to the classical tradition and staffed predominantly by Catholic clergymen, the colleges, as Roger Magnuson notes, 'offered a program of studies that was inspired and rooted in the scholastic philosophy of St. Thomas Aquinas and rounded off by the humanistic teachings of the Renaissance.' So demanding was the curriculum that, in their upper years, the colleges provided a course of study equivalent to that of a general Bachelor of Arts university program. Though predominantly arts-oriented, the colleges did not ignore the world of industry. Indeed, by 1900, one-third of their enrolments were in the commercial program, where students 'followed courses in English, arithmetic, bookkeeping, business law and banking administration.'

Heavily influenced by the entrance requirements of universities, Canadian high schools in the late nineteenth century were attended by a select constituency of Canadian youth. In 1900, fewer than 10 per cent of fifteen- to nineteen-year-olds were attending high school in English Canada. Many of these institutions still charged tuition fees, and they attracted youth primarily from middle-class families whose sons were destined for the professions and whose daughters, if they were later employed at all, would likely teach school prior to marriage. Commercial and vocational training had received some attention in Canadian high schools, a tendency, as we shall see, that would become a trend before the First World War.

Even more exclusive than public secondary schooling, however, were private, or 'independent,' schools, which continued to occupy a confined but notable space in the world of Canadian education. Mostly initiated by the wealthy patrons of the various Christian denominations, they were sustained by parents who were unimpressed by the supposed virtues of state-run schooling, and who had the resources to offer their children a select alternative. Among the oldest in the country was Stanstead College in Quebec (initiated in 1817), which provided advanced schooling for male and female Protestant youth. Its curriculum in the 1870s included the first two years of undergraduate education equivalent to that offered at McGill University, a teacher-training program, and a commercial course, the latter of which was open only to men as part of their preparation for the business world. The most prominent of Canada's nineteenth-century private schools was Upper Canada College, in Toronto, which catered to boys from the community's 'leading' families, and benefited from public subsidies, a practice which was frequently criticized. Modelled on the prestigious British boys and ladies schools, these Canadian institutions – and others such as Trinity College School, in Port Hope, Ontario; Rothesay Collegiate School, in Rothesay, New Brunswick; Halifax Ladies' School; and University School, in Victoria, British Columbia (est. 1907) – promoted Christian values, classical learning, patriotism, and character development. Males were subjected to a strong dose of athleticism, intended to inspire 'schoolboy honour,' and females studied art and music, designed to provide them with a veneer of middle-class refinement.

Its self-conscious élitism notwithstanding, private education furnished genuine educational possibilities for women who were not always well served by public schooling. We have seen how provincial authorities initially discouraged girls from enrolling in Ontario grammar schools. This induced some of the educationally ambitious to look elsewhere, including to women's 'seminaries,' of which there were seven in Ontario by the 1880s. These schools, most of which were initiated by evangelical Protestants, supported advanced, 'useful' education for women, who, as Johanna M. Selles notes, were then expected to contribute to the spiritual and cultural uplifting of society. Alma College, in St Thomas, Ontario, established in 1871 by Bishop Carman of the Methodist Episcopal Church, offered a high level of academic, artistic, and commercial studies that graduates were able to apply in the working world, particularly in teaching. Affiliated with the University of Toronto, which essentially set its curriculum, the school provided a course of study equivalent to that of a junior college.

Nor, as Nancy Jackson and Jane Gaskell maintain, should the entrepreneurially driven commercial colleges, which women began attending in the late nineteenth and early twentieth centuries, be overlooked. The British American Commercial College established a school in Toronto in 1860, where it taught penmanship, phonography (shorthand), commercial arithmetic, commercial law, and bookkeeping. It soon opened five additional colleges throughout Ontario; also created (in 1887) was the Central Business College, in Toronto, the predecessor of the well-known Shaw Business Colleges. The lukewarm reception of public secondary schools to commercial training, the short duration of the business-college courses, and the 'practical value' of their programs which qualified women for clerical and related vocations appealed to occupationally bound students. Lacking the status of secondary schools, these institutes nevertheless helped equip graduates with the means to lead more independent lives than those conventionally prescribed for young women in the late Victorian era.

Finally, Catholic academies, convents, and female boarding-schools, particularly in Quebec, were a source of educational opportunity for women with limited prospects elsewhere. Barred from classical colleges and most professions, French-Canadian women, in growing numbers, entered convents, which provided both social respectability and legitimate vocational pathways in teaching, the clergy, or the social services. Between 1841 and 1920, some 150 convent schools were founded by the Congrégation de Notre-Dame, 59 of which were outside Quebec. In 1888, some 10,000 girls in Quebec were attending 'pensionnats,' or boarding-schools, run by nuns. As Marta Danylewycz observes, the women who taught in these institutions had more autonomy and better prospects for advancement than were available to them in male-dominated schools and workplaces.

A useful, if imperfect, reflection of the impact of nineteenth-century schooling on Canadian lives was the changing literacy rate. If literacy is defined as the ability to read and write, researchers have yet to employ definitive methods for measuring it. One important documentary source retained by churches and used by historians in Canada and elsewhere are marriage registers, which include bride and bridegroom signatures. By counting the number of married adults who were able to sign their names, historians are then able to estimate quantitatively a community's level of literacy. Single adults, however, were omitted from these records, and thus not included in the calculation. Furthermore, one might have learned how to sign one's name without mastering any other literacy skills, thus diminishing the reliability of this system of measurement.

Beginning in 1861, census takers provided another source of information by asking Canadians to report on the number of household members who were able to read and write. Owing to evident confusion among enumerators, some of whom asked whether citizens could read 'or' write, later censuses posed an additional question – who could 'read only'? – leaving observers to determine whether this skill alone qualified one as literate. Historians have also used more informal methods for judging a community's level of literacy, such as the changing circulation rates of newspapers or the growth of city libraries. Always elusive in literacy studies is the question of a 'literate' individual's level of comprehension. As we have seen, Canadian schools in the nineteenth century placed great emphasis on the quality of a student's oral expression. Reciting words may have mattered more than reading for meaning. Historian Harvey Graff claims that students could 'prattle through their lessons and be promoted through the system' without necessary reference to their intelligence or actual knowledge.

Despite these conceptual and methodological dilemmas, scholars generally perceive a connection between a community's level of literacy, however it is gauged, and the state of its schooling. Canadian literacy levels showed a marked improvement in the last half of the nineteenth century, signalling, presumably, the effect of the spread of public education. In Nova Scotia, for example, the census found that, in 1861, more than 28 per cent of the population was unable to read, compared with 14 per cent in 1901 – the national average. There were, however, sharp regional differences in illiteracy rates. The low was Ontario, at 8.8 per cent, and the high was the 'Territories' (Alberta and Saskatchewan), at 31.3 per cent. In the mid-nineteenth century, as Allan Greer, and Chad Gaffield and Gérard Bouchard, note, proportionately fewer people in French-speaking Quebec could read than was the case elsewhere in Canada, though the gap had practically disappeared by the end of the century. Newfoundland, too, as David Alexander and Phillip McCann have observed, had an especially high rate of illiteracy throughout the nineteenth century. Explaining such regional differences is challenging, and requires attention to economic, cultural, and demographic factors. Ontario's pace-setting literacy rate was in all likelihood the combined result of the strong emphasis placed by evangelical Protestants on the importance of Bible reading; the major initiatives in public schooling taken by the province beginning in the 1840s; and the diversification and industrialization of the economy in the last quarter of the century, which required a better-educated population. By contrast, Newfoundland, a relatively poor fishing colony in which large numbers of children worked, generated insufficient revenue for the support of education, a problem exacerbated by the denominationally controlled school system. According to Phillip McCann, to meet the interests of competing religious sects, there was a 'proliferation [and duplication] of inferior schools,' which both consumed scarce resources and compounded the problem of poor student retention rates. While the Catholic Church in Quebec stressed the importance of training clergy, and thus extended classical education, it devoted less attention in the first half of the nineteenth century to elementary schooling, which might account for the province's relatively low level of literacy. Historians have also debated the degree to which literacy contributed to social and economic mobility. Harvey Graff has argued that, at mid-century, class and ethnic background affected one's prospects for occupational and social advancement more than did one's ability to read and write. By contrast, Gordon Darroch and Lee Soltow demonstrate that literate men in Ontario (1871) had accumulated significantly more wealth and property than their illiterate counterparts. They also show that, in general, foreign-born residents were more literate than the

Canadian-born. Clearly, questions remain about the complex but fascinating subject of the link between schooling, literacy, and social life in nineteenth-century Canada.

Key components of modern schooling were in place in Canada by the beginning of the twentieth century. Most boys and girls were now expected to spend their early educational years in state-funded and -administered schools, where they would, ideally, be prepared to take their place in the community as productive, upright citizens. Teachers increasingly taught within formal settings, featuring facilities and pedagogies intended both to extend and to regulate the students' mental development. Educational officials invariably claimed to be implementing policy on the basis of social consensus.

But, as we have seen, these goals were easier to articulate than consistently to realize. While lurching towards respectability, teachers, particularly women, often endured severe working conditions, and many earned minimal salaries. In crowded classrooms with crammed curricula, what students learned – even those who behaved – undoubtedly fell well short of what they were taught. Parents could both defer to the authority of the schoolmaster and denounce the obtuseness and insensitivity of politicians and educators. At the end of the century, what Canadian schooling had yet to achieve was at least as impressive as what it had thus far accomplished.

4

Race and Culture

How should public schools address the question of cultural difference? When classrooms include students whose religious, ethnic, or racial origins set them apart from the mainstream, what bearing should this have on educational practice? An influential – and widely debated – contemporary response is the policy of multiculturalism, which encourages minority populations to preserve their heritage while contributing to a common Canadian nationality, and educational programs designed to meet these objectives have been introduced in recent years. In the nineteenth century, Canadians were cognizant of cultural differences among them. We have seen how schooling policy – indeed, Confederation itself – sought to address the particular educational interests of Protestants and Catholics, and of French and English Canadians. But other groups reflecting the population's diversity – Native peoples, blacks, and a new wave of European immigrants – were subject to educational edicts that stressed the virtues of cultural uniformity over cultural accommodation. Voices promoting the principles of equality and liberality were periodically heard, and some schools did foster ethnic and linguistic protectionism. More commonly, educational policy governing minority populations was driven by paternalism, prejudice, and political expediency. The ideals, let alone the practices, of the multicultural mosaic had yet to take root.

When the British Crown assumed control of the territory previously known as New France, Native peoples acquired a political master whose language differed from but whose message echoed that of its predecessor. English-speaking authorities, fur traders, and missionaries hoped to secure the peace and prosperity of British North America by subduing, negotiating with, and Christianizing the Indian population. In the late eighteenth and early nineteenth centuries, military and economic concerns were the Crown's chief priorities. Native alliances played an important strategic role during the American Revolution, and again in the War of 1812; not surprisingly, military rather than civil authority governed Native affairs in the British colonies during this period. Aboriginals, too, had long been vital to the success of the fur trade, which in 1821 fell under the monopoly of the Hudson's Bay Company. So long as they served such practical imperatives, the colonial government devoted minimal attention to the matter of aboriginal culture and education, leaving initiatives in these realms to Protestant and Catholic missionaries who continued their earnest quest to 'save' Native souls.

As the threat of war receded, as the fur trade entered a long decline, and as white settlement encroached on Indian areas, especially in Upper Canada, the future of aboriginal communities assumed new significance. Having surrendered or sold the bulk of their land to the British in exchange for material requirements, the Natives of the provinces were beset by uncertainty, ill health, and economic insecurity. The Upper-Canadian response, later emulated elsewhere, was to move Indians to reserves and attempt to educate them in day schools run by the churches, where they would be taught skills designed to facilitate their assimilation into a non-Native world. To expedite the process, responsibility for Native affairs in each of the colonies was officially transferred from the military to the civilian authority in 1830. Sir George Murray, secretary of state for the colonies, explained that the policy had the purpose of 'gradually reclaiming the Indians from a state of barbarism and introducing amongst them the industrious and peaceful habits of civilized life.'

Among the earliest evangelical efforts had been that of the New England Company, a non-sectarian Protestant organization, which in 1797 established the mission school of Sussex Vale near present-day Saint John, New Brunswick. Lured by the promise of economic security, poor Native children expected that the apprenticeship training offered by the 'Indian College' would lead to occupational self-sufficiency. The 'students,' however, received virtually no academic instruction and were assigned to farmers who were paid by the company to teach them agricultural skills. But as historian J.R. Miller notes, 'the so-called apprenticeship system often turned out to be nothing but a system of providing Euro-Canadian farmers with labour that was not only free but subsidized.' A report in the 1820s condemned the school as a 'disastrous failure' which left the children largely untrained and subjected to abuse, both economically and physically. The school closed in 1826.

Along with other missionaries, the New England Company turned its attention to the rapidly growing territory of Upper Canada. Reflecting the fervency of their revivalist campaigns, Methodists were especially active in Native education there, having set up eleven schools for some 400 students by 1830. Organizers of the Credit River School, attended by Mississauga students, hoped to convert them to Christianity, teach them how to farm, and diminish the influence in their lives of traditional Native practices. Symbolizing these goals was this instruction posted on the schoolhouse wall: 'No blanket to be worn in school.'

A leading figure among Methodist educators was Reverend Peter Jones, the son of an Ojibwa woman who had been married to a white government surveyor. Also known as Kahkewaquonaby, Jones converted to Christianity, and in

1850 established the Mount Elgin Industrial school for Natives, at the Munceytown Reserve. The concept of 'industrial schooling,' which was inspired by an American Presbyterian missionary working earlier in the century among the Cherokee, was embraced enthusiastically in 1847 by Egerton Ryerson, Ontario's superintendent of education. Intended to 'raise the Tribes within the British Territory to the level of their White neighbours,' these schools were expected to teach manual and domestic skills to Native students. For boys, 'husbandry, gardening, the management of stock, and simple mechanical trades' were recommended; girls were to be taught 'domestic economy, the charge of household and dairy, the use of the needle'; 'and both sexes should be familiarized with the mode of transacting business among the whites.'

Residential schools, away from the reserves, were the preferred venue for this form of instruction. Acknowledging the partial success of religious-conversion campaigns, government officials remained frustrated by the continuing refusal of most Natives to abandon their customs and communities. According to a provincial committee investigating Indian affairs, only if Native children were 'weaned from the habits and feelings of their ancestors' could they be expected to thrive in a European-based civilization. The less contact students had with their families, the more likely they were to escape their influence.

This model of Native education, which included residential and day schools, endured throughout Canada for the remainder of the nineteenth century, though important administrative changes with respect to Native affairs were made at the time of Confederation. To facilitate its anticipated control of western lands, to which Natives had increasingly retreated in the face of white settlement, the federal government, under the terms of the British North America Act, assumed full responsibility for aboriginal matters. The Indian Act of 1876 and 1880 consolidated this system by placing social services, including the provision of education, in federal hands, essentially making Indians 'wards of the federal government.'

Industrial schools where students boarded were designed to hasten Native assimilation by addressing academic, occupational, and behavioural concerns. European dress and hairstyles, the use of the English language, and obedience to authority were all required. The curriculum, generally confined to basic education, included a half-day of manual labour in agriculture, crafts, or household duties meant to prepare pupils, in the words of historians Jean Barman, Yvonne Hébert, and Don McCaskill, 'for their future existence on the lower fringes of the dominant society.'

One of the first such schools, Shingwauk Industrial Home, founded by Anglican missionary Edward F. Wilson in 1873 near Sault Ste Marie, embodied these pedagogical principles. Intended for the 'civilization, education and Christian training of Indian children,' the school was initially supported by the two leading Ojibwa chiefs in the region, Shingwauk and his brother Buhkwujjenene. So committed were they to its prospects for success that they placed their own children in the school, hoping that they would 'learn to gain [their] living in the same way as the white people.'

As prescribed, Shingwauk prohibited students from talking in their native Ojibway tongue (except at teatime). While other schools simply punished students for violating this rule, Shingwauk's approach was more inventive. Each week students were given buttons, one of which would be taken from them every time they spoke in their Native language. At the end of the week, those left with the most buttons could exchange them for nuts. Another alternative to corporal punishment designed to induce compliance with authority was the use of 'pressure and shame.' Cards would be publicly exhibited identifying those who had displayed good and bad conduct, and placing the names of the latter on the 'Black list.'

Despite such innovations, the school faced many prob-

lems. As historian J. Donald Wilson notes, it was frequently
underenrolled, and homesick, bored, or rebellious children often ran away – sometimes temporarily, sometimes
for good. Those who remained completed on average less
than two years of the five-year program. Graduates, including those with applied skills, rarely moved into the white
community. Instead they returned to the reserve and stayed
there. Even the school's founder, Edward Wilson, became
disillusioned, and by the 1890s he had lost faith in the
prospects of assimilation and had begun promoting Native
autonomy. The Indian, he claimed, 'views everything that
the white man does for him with suspicion, believing that
this hated policy for the absorption of his race and his
nationality is at the back of it.'

Wilson's reformed views, however, were atypical. Inspired
by a commissioned report in 1879, which enthused over the
American system of residential schools, particularly those
offering 'industrial' education, the federal government al-
lotted funds in 1883 for the establishment of three such
facilities, two in Saskatchewan, at Qu'Appelle and Battle-
ford, and one in Alberta, at High River. Government subsidies for the construction and maintenance of the schools
would be augmented by contributions from the churches,
which were assigned responsibility for managing the institutions and teaching the students. The system expanded, so
that by 1902, there were 22 industrial schools, the majority
in the prairies, each controlled by the Catholic, Anglican,
Methodist, or Presbyterian Church. In addition, there were
40 boarding-schools for young Native youth, and 221 day
schools for those living on reserves, scattered across the
country.

According to several case-studies, the residential schools
had similar goals, challenges, and quandaries. They continued to stress the importance of isolating children from
their families; they demeaned Indian customs and promoted Christian values; they engaged students in English
games, including cricket and soccer; and they required

practical 'training,' which for many students involved little more than working in the garden or cleaning the school-house. The academic curriculum was similar to that offered in public schools, but as historians E. Brian Titley and Jean Barman note, the students' work details meant that they received only half the classroom instruction of that provided to non-Natives. Many of the instructors were Church-appointed volunteers lacking the academic background of public-school teachers. And the schools also faced chronic funding shortages, securing far less income than those in the provincial public systems.

Discipline was a continuing concern and, in the most extreme cases, brutally administered. Reports of physical mistreatment, of 'thrashings and whippings,' damaged the reputation of Rupert's Land Indian School, in Manitoba, and in 1899 its principal was replaced after physically and sexually abusing several children. Angered also by the 'unpaid labour' required of students, a number of parents withdrew their children from the school in the early 1890s. Nor were health conditions ideal at Rupert's Land or elsewhere. In 1893, seven of twenty-three girls who had left the school died of unspecified causes. The incidence of contagious disease was especially high in Native schools. A government report noted that 28 per cent of the students who attended Sarcee Boarding School, in Alberta, between 1894 and 1908 had died, primarily from tuberculosis. According to historian J.R. Miller, 'by the early twentieth century the escalating death rates in the schools were becoming a public scandal as well as a reason for both parental and student refusal to cooperate with the residential schooling experiment.'

Somewhat more positive was the early experience of All Hallows School for girls, founded in 1884 in the Yale District of British Columbia. Unlike other residential schools, it was attended by both Native and non-Native students, the latter of whom were seeking a high-quality Christian education unavailable in the province's non-denominational school system. At the same time, the school afforded Indian children a rare opportunity to be educated on the same terms as whites. Originally taught together, the children were segregated in 1890, after some white parents objected to mixed classes, and the students' shared activities diminished to a daily religious service. Still, according to federal assessments, the Native pupils performed exceedingly well. A visitor to the school in 1895 reported in 'astonishment' that two Indian girls had become so proficient that they were teaching other students regularly.

Unfortunately, after the turn of the century, the quality of Native schooling at All Hallows deteriorated, the result, in part, of a change in federal government policy affecting Indian education across the country. In 1897, Clifford Sifton, the new federal minister of the interior in the Laurier Liberal government, declared the residential-school system a failure, blamed Indians for its demise, and deplored its continuing consumption of public revenues. Natives, he believed, lacked 'the physical, mental, or moral get up' of whites and could never compete with them on equal terms. A moratorium was declared on the building of residential schools, and their funding, never abundant, was reduced. In 1910, the curricula of the schools was further 'simplified,' officially providing the bare essentials of academic instruction. School attendance for Natives was made mandatory in 1920 – an 1894 compulsory-schooling regulation was notoriously unsuccessful – but positive results of the new law were hard to divine. As late as 1951, 40 per cent of Indians in Canada over the age of five, according to the census, had no formal schooling.

By most measures, Native schooling – particularly of the residential variety – failed to achieve its objectives, which themselves were questionable. Confining Indian students to Native-only schools offering inferior education could hardly facilitate assimilation. Promoting a model of assimilation which required aboriginal youth to abandon their communities and repudiate their heritage was problematic on both ethical and practical grounds. And, as Jean Barman contends, a policy which ignored the 'diversity and individuality' of Natives, and which 'simply reduced them to a single dependent status,' was paternalistic in the extreme.

At the same time, as J.R. Miller suggests, the coercive power of the schools was probably limited. Chronically under-enrolled, they reached a small proportion of the total Native population. Only 6,127 of 123,589 Indians in Canada in 1888 were attending any kind of educational institution, and truant students were usually difficult to track down. Nor were most students kept away from their families for long periods of time. As we have seen, the majority who attended were in day schools or boarding-schools, situated on or close to the reserves, not in the more elaborate industrial schools located much farther from their homes. It should also be remembered, as Miller and John Webster Grant point out, that, in a number of cases, Indian bands themselves supported the schools and petitioned for their creation in the hope of enhancing their children's life chances. Indeed, in the late 1890s, Shoal Lake Ojibwas played a major role in the establishment and administration of Cecilia Jeffrey School in Kenora, Ontario. In other instances, the families resisted authority and asserted some influence by 'protesting, petitioning, sending children to competing institutions, or boycotting schools altogether.' A great irony of twentieth-century residential schooling is that its graduates included prominent leaders of the aboriginal-rights movement whose educational experiences fuelled their political activism. Native peoples may not have derived significant benefit from the schooling they endured in the nineteenth and early twentieth centuries, but neither were they completely its captives. The fundamental problem – the marginalization of First Nations' society and culture – predated the schools, and survived them.

Though associated primarily with the American South, slavery endured in the British colonies in the eighteenth and early nineteenth centuries, as it had earlier during the French regime, and was not officially abolished in the British Empire until 1833. Brought to Nova Scotia by New England settlers in the 1750s and by Loyalist immigrants after the American Revolution, black slaves numbered some 1,500 by the early 1780s. In addition, as part of the British plan to debilitate the economy of the Southern states, and to recruit labour for the British forces, some 3,000 'emancipated' blacks were drawn to the colonies, mainly to Nova Scotia, in 1783. Granted far less land by the British government than that received by white Loyalists, blacks in Nova Scotia endured poverty and discrimination, a condition that was reflected in the poor quality of schooling they received throughout the nineteenth century.

A second wave of American blacks came to the Maritimes and Upper Canada during the War of 1812, when the British government offered to free all slaves who deserted their American masters. Slavery again drove blacks to Canada after 1850, when the Fugitive Slave Law rendered the Northern American states as dangerous to fleeing slaves as was the South. Concentrated in a number of communities in Nova Scotia and Ontario, in the 1850s blacks comprised some 8 per cent of the population of Halifax, and more than half the population in some communities around the city. Between one-fifth and one-third of the residents of Chatham, Amherstburg, and Colchester in southwestern Ontario were black.

In the era before the rise of public schooling, black children in Nova Scotia and Ontario were educated, if at all, in philanthropic or missionary schools run by organizations such as the Society for the Propagation of the Gospel. A notable initiative had been taken in 1813 by a retired officer, Captain Walter Henry Bromley, who opened a Lancasterian monitorial school for poor whites, blacks, and Mi'kmaq Indians in Halifax. On occasion, common schools were effectively integrated, such as the Buxton School, near Chatham, Ontario, whose academic reputation was so high by the 1850s that it drew students from as far away as the United States. But this was an exception. In the face of thriving prejudice, 'coloured' children were almost always unwelcome and were normally educated in segregated black-only schools.

So opposed were white Canadians to the 'mixing' of the races that provincial laws legitimized the practice of 'separate' schooling under the guise of respecting minority rights. In Canada West, the Separate School Act of 1850 provided that any group of five black families could petition for a separate 'coloured' school, which in practice enabled white parents and trustees to bar or oust black children from common schools anywhere that an alternative facility existed or could be created. The Nova Scotian law permitted school commissioners of any municipality to 'establish separate schools if they, rather than a body of petitioners, thought them necessary and if the government approved.' Several attempts – all unsuccessful – were made to force the withdrawal of this legislation, though in 1884 an amendment guaranteed blacks admission to common schools where separate teaching facilities were unavailable. As Robin Winks notes, this had the effect of strengthening segregated schools in Nova Scotian communities heavily populated by blacks, and of preventing segregation in those areas where their numbers were small.

So intense was the hostility to integrated schooling in the town of Amherstburg, Canada West, that white citizens reportedly promised to 'cut their children's heads off and throw them into the road side ditch' if they were forced to attend school 'with niggers.' In the early 1860s, the local school in Chatham, which once had fifty students, was left with an enrolment of nine – seven of whom were black – after white parents who opposed integration withdrew their children. In the community of Harwich, whites voted in the 1860s to establish a separate school for blacks, but could not afford to hire two common-school teachers. Absurdly, the single teacher was expected to move throughout the day between the two adjacent schools.

Unable to secure a change in the law, blacks were thus compelled to establish schools for their own children. Mary Bibb, a black American immigrant, came to Canada West in 1850, and over the next two decades operated a number of institutions, some of which she had to close down for lack of adequate funding. Not all black parents opposed segregated schooling. However inadequate the facilities, students attending them would at least be free of racial taunts and taught in a more receptive environment. Indeed, as Paul Bennett notes, Amherstburg's King Street School for blacks became in the 1880s a 'hub of children's activity,' a social and recreational centre featuring concerts, dances, and boxing matches, and the home of a literary society devoted to community 'self-improvement.'

Egerton Ryerson deplored the public attitudes that sustained racially divided schools, but his office was unable, or unwilling, to surmount the bigotry of parents and educators. He claimed, in deferring to local demands, that however 'unchristian,' 'prejudice ... is stronger than law itself.' The 1850 legislation stood, and while segregated schooling gradually lost favour in the decades that followed, the policy facilitating it remained officially on the books until 1964. Ontario's last segregated black school, in Colchester, was finally shut down in 1965. The Nova Scotian law supporting segregated schooling lapsed in 1954.

The experiences of aboriginals and black Canadians illustrated a paradox that bedevilled the country through the late nineteenth and early twentieth centuries. Educators, politicians, and religious leaders stressed the virtues of a unified national culture in a way that appeared to diminish the status of certain minority groups. On the one hand, the concept of assimilation suggested inclusiveness and social equality; on the other hand, it privileged Canada's dominant racial, ethnic, linguistic, and religious communities. As the nation's population grew and diversified, the tensions deepened and spilled into the realm of schooling.

Perhaps the best-known, and most-studied, of these conflicts was the one which erupted in Manitoba in 1890, when the provincial government abolished the dual school system (Catholic and Protestant) and replaced it with a single regime of public schools. As we noted in chapter 2, denominational education had been guaranteed by the British North America Act to those religious groups benefiting from such schooling at the time their provinces joined Confederation. Since 1870, when the Métis-dominated province of Manitoba was created, the composition of the population changed dramatically. By the 1880s, it had become, in historian Gerald Friesen's term, a 'British-Ontario' community, comprising in the main English-speaking Protestants who were determined to create educational institutions which best met their perceived needs. They believed that publicly funded Catholic schools, in which students studied largely in French, were costly impediments to the task of forging a culture rooted in Anglo-Saxon traditions and values. Many French Canadians, on the other hand, saw the eradication of bilingual Catholic schools, in Manitoba and other provinces, as an affront both to their legal rights and to their dignity, and a challenge to their understanding of the fundamental purpose of Confederation. They and their anglophone supporters contended that the whole of Canada ought to be culturally hospitable to French and English Canadians alike.

Intolerance clearly contributed to the strife in Manitoba, typified most dramatically by an incendiary speech delivered in Portage la Prairie in 1889 by D'Alton McCarthy, a Toronto lawyer and leader of the Equal Rights Association, an organization devoted to eliminating the 'special privi-

leges' of Roman Catholics throughout Canada. Equally provocative rhetoric flowed from the editorial pages of some
Ontario newspapers in the 1880s, one of which described
the bilingual separate schools of Russell and Prescott counties as 'nurseries ... of an alien tongue ... alien customs ...
alien sentiments, and we say without offense, a wholly alien
people.' The migration of French Canadians to eastern
Ontario and of English Canadians to Manitoba led to
greater contact between culturally distinct communities,
and tested their ability to resolve their differences without
rancour.

For some historians, however, bigotry only partly explains
the Manitoba and Ontario school conflicts. In the former
case, local concerns about the quality and costs of schooling
lay behind the controversial 1890 legislation. As Tom
Mitchell explains, the growth of Brandon's non-Catholic
population led to overcrowding in the community's Protestant school even as scarce tax dollars were still supporting
the underenrolled Catholic school. Ending duplication,
generating greater efficiency, and improving the overall
level of instruction in Brandon and elsewhere thus required
and justified a revamping of the system, and provincial
politicians frequently made the case on these grounds.

Still, the constitutional question, addressed on the national stage, dominated the debate throughout the 1890s.
Following several court challenges, the defeat of the Conservative government, and the victory of the Liberal party
under Prime Minister Wilfrid Laurier, a compromise was
reached in 1897 which restored Catholic educational rights
without resurrecting the denominational-school system.
Catholic teachers would be hired where the Catholic
student population was significant in size, and, upon the
request of ten families, religious instruction would be provided at the end of the school day. Furthermore, instruction in French or any other non-English tongue was
permitted where these were the spoken languages of ten or
more students.

The campaign to eliminate bilingual schooling in Ontario culminated in 1912 with the imposition of Regulation 17, which barred schools from using French as the language of instruction beyond the first two grades. (The legislation was made somewhat less restrictive in 1913.) Here, too, while pro-Imperialist, anti-French rhetoric was rife, particularly in light of an aggressive movement by the French-Canadian Association of Ontario to expand French-based teaching in the province, ethnic differences accounted for some but not all of the conflict.

Chad Gaffield attributes tensions in eastern Ontario between English- and French-speaking residents to insecurities generated by changing economic conditions in the last half of the nineteenth century. Seldom a preoccupation in stable times, the school question became an outlet for the expression of social and class divisions in an era when employment prospects were less predictable. So, too, in justifying Regulation 17, proponents questioned the ability of bilingual schools to equip Franco-Ontarian youth for employment in the modern industrial world. Many of the students spoke no English, attended class infrequently, and were taught by some of the least qualified and most poorly paid teachers in the province. As Robert Stamp notes, reforms were considered necessary to bring these schools into the 'mainstream of educational development.' However legitimate such arguments, cultural concerns – and invective – fuelled the educational debate, especially in the midst of the First World War, when relations between French and English Canadians descended to new depths.

However contentious were the subjects of separate schools and French-language education, they had held, since Confederation, a type of special status on the minority-rights agenda. But the influx of immigrants from parts of Europe where French and English were unspoken and where Christianity was not universally practised led the educational debate into uncharted waters at the turn of the century. If the cultures represented by newcomers were unfamiliar to most Canadians, the assimilationist strategies proferred by politicians and educators were not without precedent.

The growing diversity of the Canadian population arose from the long-delayed success of a national policy intended to settle the West with experienced farmers from abroad. While small communities of Mennonites, Icelanders, and Jews had established prairie homesteads before 1890, the territory remained sparsely inhabited in comparison with the more prosperous and alluring American West. Between 1900 and 1914, however, the tide turned, and Canada attracted more than 1.5 million immigrants, half of whom settled in the prairies. The saturation of the American frontier, the displacement of European farmers and workers by the forces of industrialization, and the implementation of an aggressive overseas recruitment strategy by the federal government after 1896 contributed to this population surge, which was felt as well in major urban centres. Among the largest communities of European immigrants settling on the prairies were Germans, Scandinavians, and Ukrainians. The resource and railway frontiers drew Italian migrants, and Jews congregated primarily in Montreal, Toronto, and Winnipeg. Chinese immigrants who had been hired as railway workers in the 1880s later resided primarily in Vancouver.

The newcomers encountered an environment that was at once receptive and hostile. Employers were eager to exploit immigrant labour, and consumers devoured the high-quality grain profitably transported by rail from prairie farmlands. The prosperity of Canada at the turn of the century obviously owed much to the productivity of its agricultural and industrial workers, so many of whom were recent arrivals.

But their alien languages and customs were frequently scorned by other Canadians who mistrusted, and made little effort to understand, the unfamiliar. Nativist or racist attitudes were reflected in new immigration regulations (1906–10) designed to preserve the 'national fabric' of Canada by limiting, or halting, the influx of Slavs, Orientals, and East Indians, and by luring those of British origin. Moulded by hereditarian and social Darwinist thinking, which ranked races according to their supposed genetic qualities, Canadian policy now gave preference to immigrants from northern climates, who were considered more durable and reliable than those from the south. Select groups of Caucasian migrants were thus beckoned to Canada; blacks and other 'coloureds' were thwarted or banned. Among the most extreme acts of domestic intolerance was an anti-Asian riot which erupted in Vancouver in 1907. As historians Robert Harney and Harold Troper note, for most Canadians 'the foreign issue boiled down to one single problem – why can't they be like us?'

Schools were intended to make 'them' so. To address the challenge posed by what David Goggin, superintendent of schools in the Northwest Territories, called a 'foreign and relatively ignorant population,' immigrant children were to be taught to 'adopt our viewpoint and speak our speech.' From prairie schoolhouses to Ontario's urban classrooms, new Canadians encountered, in Luigi Pennacchio's term, the 'four cornerstones' of British-Canadian citizenship: Imperial patriotism, Protestantism, the English language, and cleanliness. Children learned the words to 'Rule Britannia' and, with their English-speaking schoolmates, participated in regular Bible readings. Arithmetic courses stressed the virtues of 'growth, progress, and competitive business practices,' and school texts reinforced the message of Anglo-Saxon superiority. *The Dominion School Geography,* used in British Columbia's elementary schools between 1911 and 1923, described the 'White Race' as the most active, enterprising, and intelligent race in the world.' By contrast, 'The Yellow Race' comprised 'some of the [world's] most backward tribes ..., and as a rule, [is] not progressive.'

The goal of assimilation, in a climate of paternalism, thus informed the schooling of immigrant children in the period preceding the First World War. But this was not the whole story, particularly on the prairies. As we noted earlier, the regulations flowing from the resolution of the Manitoba Schools conflict included a clause which permitted students, where their numbers justified, to be taught in languages other than English. Because the 1897 act predated the influx of European immigrants, provincial authorities anticipated that only French Canadians would make use of the new educational law. But other groups did too, including Mennonites, Poles, and especially Ukrainians, who by 1915 had established some 400 'bilingual' schools in the West, primarily in Manitoba, which provided English and Ukrainian instruction. So popular was this form of schooling that the provincial government opened a 'Ruthenian' training school in Winnipeg in 1905 designed to increase the supply of Ukrainian-English and Polish-English bilingual teachers. As Stella Hryniuk and Neil McDonald conclude, the schools signalled both the commitment of Ukrainian parents to improved education and their quest for a more culturally sensitive route to assimilation.

Saskatchewan and Alberta authorized separate schooling and, with somewhat less latitude than Manitoba, made provision for non-English instruction. But, as in Ontario, the currents promoting cultural uniformity, fanned by the First World War, swept across the prairies, and, by 1918, bilingual schooling was virtually eliminated in all three provinces.

As non-Christians, Canadian Jews were both a cultural and a religious minority. To equip their children for the future, Jewish parents willingly enrolled them in public schools. But to protect its cultural identity, the community established Jewish education programs to which children were sent at the end of the public-school day. 'Talmud/Torah' classes reflected the diversity of the commuity itself – pro-Zionist, pro-socialist, Yiddish, Hebrew, religious or secular in their orientation. What most Jews shared were experiences of discrimination, highlighted by regulations in Montreal which denied Jews the right to teach in or serve on the Protestant School Board, notwithstanding the fact that, by 1916, Jewish youth comprised nearly half of the 22,000 students in the system.

In spite of such efforts to repress it, ethnic pluralism survived in Canada, in part because schools and other Canadianization agencies – ironically – were forever reminding immigrant workers and farmers of their cultural differences. Canadians claimed to favour the assimilation of foreigners, but they did not want to live among them. Consequently, enclosed communities, such as the 'Ward' in Toronto, occupied by Jews, developed thriving cultural lives of their own, where religious schooling, social activities, small businesses, and mutual-aid societies made the difficult transition to the 'Canadian way' less arduous. Both in school and out, Canada's newest residents learned a lesson already known by some of its oldest – aboriginals, blacks, and francophones: the minority presence, and the condescension that greeted it, were fixtures of the urban and rural landscape.

5

Higher Learning

By the late nineteenth century, universities provided the most select type of formal schooling available in Canada. Drawn increasingly from the small ranks of youth who had obtained a secondary-school education, the university-trained were well positioned for occupational and community roles that promised social prestige and relative security. As distant as they were from the lives of most Canadians, universities were not unmoved by the currents of change that flowed through other institutions, including common schools. The product initially of sacred visions and sectarian interests, they had by century's end been stirred by the spirit of science, the aura of the secular, and the values of the marketplace.

As we noted in chapter 1, in the early nineteenth century the forces of Christianity and loyalism spurred schooling initiatives, including those in the realm of higher education. The Anglican-dominated King's College of New Brunswick, Nova Scotia, and, later, Upper Canada, were designed to provide the colonies with clergymen and community leaders who would inspire fidelity both to God and to the British Empire. This mission, however, failed to address the religious needs of an increasingly diverse, though still unmistakably Christian, population. Institutions such as Acadia, in Wolfville, Nova Scotia (Baptist); St Mary's, in Halifax (Catholic); Mount Allison, in Sackville, New Brunswick (Methodist); Bishop's, in Lennoxville, Quebec (Anglican); Laval, in Quebec City (Catholic); Ottawa (Catholic); Queen's, in Kingston, Ontario (Presbyterian); Victoria, in Cobourg, Ontario (Methodist); Trinity, in Toronto (Anglican); St John's, in Winnipeg (Anglican), all took root and endured. McGill University in Montreal and Dalhousie College in Halifax were both officially non-denominational but had especially close ties to the Anglican and Presbyterian communities, respectively. Students could attend two other non-denominational institutions: the University of Toronto and the University of New Brunswick (the former King's College). By 1871 there were 1,561 students in seventeen Canadian universities, the largest of which, McGill, registered 323 students; ten of the campuses had enrolments of 50 or fewer.

However earnest these institutional initiatives, the small student numbers pointed to a stark reality facing the universities: their survival was not assured. Some colleges indeed disappeared, and the prospects of those which later thrived were, at times, terribly dim. Dalhousie, for example, was 'founded' in 1818, did not enrol a single student until 1838, closed in 1845, and reopened on a continuing basis only in 1863. Religious tensions and meagre resources hampered university development in the colonies, as did the periodic problem of indifferent institutional leadership.

Dependent primarily on donations from churches, individual supporters, and affluent businessmen, Canadian universities were less successful than their American counterparts in securing reliable and continuous sources of funding. With a larger population base, a more developed business sector, and a higher proportion of educationally ambitious evangelical communities, the United States witnessed an earlier and more sustained growth of higher education. Fabulously wealthy entrepreneurs with money to spend on universities and other causes were a more visible and significant presence in the United States especially in the late nineteenth century.

Still, such individuals were not unknown in Canada, and their role in funding universities should not be overlooked. Determined to serve the educational needs of his class and community, James McGill, a prominent merchant, magistrate, and militia man in Montreal, provided the endowment which led to the founding of McGill University in 1821. Later contributions by the Molson and Redpath families, and by other anglophone business leaders, earned McGill the status of Canada's foremost private university. Dalhousie's future appeared brighter following donations in the 1880s totalling some $330,000 from George Munro, a Nova Scotian who had become a successful New York publisher. William McMaster, a devout Baptist and financier, consigned virtually his entire estate ($900,000) to the cause of a new university, founded in his name in Toronto in 1887 (and relocated in Hamilton, Ontario, in 1930).

These notable gifts notwithstanding, many Canadian universities, especially those traditionally dependent on the support of single denominations, required alternative strategies if they hoped to continue. An innovative route to this end was the scheme of university federation. Unable to survive on the basis of private or Church support and, after 1868, denied any funding from the provincial government, a number of Church-linked Ontario institutions surrendered their autonomy to the non-denominational University of Toronto. The latter had been created in 1849 as a resolution to the long-standing debate over the appropriate role of government in the support of higher learning. The new publicly funded and lay-governed university would owe allegiance to no specific religious body, though it remained committed, like public elementary schools, to upholding Christian values. Denominational colleges which affiliated with Toronto were permitted to teach theology and some arts subjects, but their students would receive University of Toronto degrees and were governed by its regulations. By the first decade of the twentieth century, five former religious colleges – including Victoria, St Michael's, and Trinity – had accepted these terms and joined the University of Toronto. Two Ontario universities which chose to remain independent – Queen's and Western Ontario – soon divested themselves of religious authority, and secularized in order to qualify for provincial funding.

A similar approach was adopted in 1877 in Manitoba, and was later emulated in the other Western provinces. Four religious colleges were the original constituent components of the non-denominational University of Manitoba, which conducted examinations and issued students their academic degrees. In Nova Scotia, an attempt at university federation in the 1870s failed, and the universities struggled independently, largely without government funding, into the twentieth century. As Peter Waite notes, religious and regional rivalries were so intense in the province that institutional cooperation, however sensible, proved impossible. In Quebec, Laval University – under Roman Catholic governance – was the centre of higher education, to which the classical colleges, the École Polytechnique, and a new higher education branch at Montreal (established in 1876), were all affiliated. Committed to competing interpretations of Catholic theology, Laval academics in Quebec City and their counterparts in Montreal were deeply divided intellectually and politically. This tension impeded the progress of higher education in French-speaking Quebec, though it also led to the establishment of the independent Université de Montréal in 1919. Thus to maintain their viability and high moral purpose in a world of scarce resources, Canadian universities in the late nineteenth century employed a variety of tools: dogmatism, pragmatism, and innovation. These strategies led in most provinces to the loosening of religious authority and the growing importance of state funding, trends that would accelerate in the more secular milieu of the early twentieth century.

What constituted higher learning in the nineteenth century? This is a complex question because the demarcation lines between secondary and 'post'-secondary education were, for the early part of this era, unclear. Advanced schooling – that which lay beyond common or elementary instruction – was offered in grammar schools, seminaries, academies, colleges, and universities. These institutions focused especially on classical studies – religion, mathematics, Latin, and Greek – and provided their graduates with a veneer of social respectability. But the admission standards varied from place to place, and, as Robert Gidney and Wyn Millar point out, the courses of study in colleges and grammar schools frequently overlapped. Indeed, in the absence of adequate grammar schooling, parents with sufficient resources might choose instead to send their sons to a college or university. And in a competitive environment with a shortage of well-educated applicants, struggling institutions such as Victoria and Queen's could scarcely 'afford to turn away any fee-paying student, however ill qualified.'

As the boundaries and curricula of secondary schooling became better defined, generally from the 1860s on, Canadian universities set clearer admission criteria. Students increasingly were expected to complete high-school 'matriculation' examinations before entering a university. Institutional overlap, however, did not disappear. Senior matriculation, or the final year of high school, was usually equivalent to the first year of university study, and high school graduates holding this qualification would enter the second year of their university program. Junior matriculants, on the other hand, would enrol in first year. By 1890, as Robin Harris explains, matriculation requirements were 'essentially the same for all Canadian institutions.' High-school graduates planning to enter university required standing in five subjects: classics, mathematics, English, history with geography, and either science or a modern language.

Once enrolled in an institution of higher learning, students, whether they realized it or not, were enveloped by an intellectual world in transition. A student pursuing a Bachelor of Arts degree in the 1850s in both French and English Canada was steeped in studies designed to refine his Christian sensibilities and prepare him for a possible career in the clergy. Science was also taught, usually under the rubric of 'natural theology,' an approach which explained the wonders of nature as a manifestation of 'God's handiwork.' French, English, and Scottish influences, reflecting the national origin and educational backgrounds of most university teachers, infused both curriculum and pedagogy. In this intellectual universe, knowledge and religion were inseparable.

The publication of Charles Darwin's major treatises, *On the Origin of Species* (1859) and *The Descent of Man* (1871), stunned the scholarly world with their contention that all species, including humans, evolved, changed, or disappeared according to observable laws of nature. This theory challenged biblical authority by questioning the story of creation, and by dating it millions of years prior to that implied in the book of Genesis. Darwin's work was the subject of fierce debate in academic circles in Canada as elsewhere because it tested the theological foundations upon which university education was built. While some scholars unconditionally repudiated Darwin's theories, others, as A.B. McKillop observes, sought an intellectual accommodation which combined spiritual and scientific principles. This balance, however, was difficult to sustain, especially in a world dazzled by revolutionary developments in medicine and technology, where God's role was not easily discernible. By the end of the century, noted a Queen's professor, the idea of evolution, 'once considered a perilous heresy ... now rank[s] among the world's most treasured conceptions,' and had found its way into Canadian university curricula.

Though it lost its authority over science, Christianity was not abandoned – on campus or off. Instead, in the work of certain influential scholars, it was adapted to the concerns of a more secular world. As McKillop notes, 'God's intentions were [now] sought less in nature than in conduct.' John Watson, a prominent philosopher at Queen's University from the early 1870s to the 1920s, articulated an 'idealistic' vision of society that linked elements of traditionalism and modernism. A devoted Christian, his notion of evolution embraced moral and social principles: like the German scholar Hegel, he believed that society was moving towards a condition of harmony that was consistent with God's will. It was thus the duty of all students – and citizens – to work for individual and social improvement. 'The aim of the university,' he wrote, was to 'produce noble, intelligent, unselfish men, and if it fails in that, it has failed in its highest vocation.'

No institution, not even high-minded universities, could fully achieve Watson's lofty ideals, but convictions such as his were used to justify a broadening of the university curriculum. Service to society could embrace an array of goals, including character development, professional training, preparation for the business world, missionary work, and community leadership. Biblical knowledge and fluency in Latin were no longer the dominant symbols of middle-class respectability, though they were still venerated components of the arts curriculum. The study of English and modern languages assumed growing importance and were now augmented by courses in Western philosophy, political economy, and history. Science specialties were found at most institutions, and professional training in medicine, engineering, education, pharmacy, dentistry, and law was more fully situated in universities, gradually replacing independent proprietary schools. The pursuit of truth through

philosophical and spiritual speculation lost ground to em-
pirical research into contemporary urban and rural problems. Reflecting the emergence of a capitalistic, industrial
order, the cleric and the classicist now shared the academic
stage with the engineer and the economist. Universities
hoped to cultivate individuals with estimable values and
useful skills. As McGill English professor Cyrus MacMillan
wrote in 1911, higher education's role 'converge[d] into
one main idea – the making of a man.'

Typically, MacMillan's comment took no account of wom-
en's presence in universities, which by 1900 constituted 11
per cent of the student enrolment. Achieving even that
proportion had been no small feat, given the opposition
aroused by the campaign to admit women to the hallowed
halls of higher learning. Mount Allison University in New
Brunswick was the country's institutional pioneer, when it
granted entry to Grace Annie Lockhart in 1872, and three
years later made her the first woman to receive a university
degree in the British Empire. Most other Canadian universities – Laval being a notable exception – opened their
doors to women over the next decade. But the arguments
against coeducation still resonated, and they were used to
justify confining university women to a limited academic
program. Full gender equality, in both curricular and extracurricular spheres, was a distant prospect.

The case against admitting women to universities, and
teaching them in the same classrooms as men, was made
most forcefully by Edward Clarke, a Harvard medical professor, in his well-known book, *Sex in Education* (1874).
Employing the authority of both religion and a version of
evolutionary science, he contended that 'identical education of the sexes is a crime before God and humanity' which
'emasculates boys and stunts girls.' In the presence of
women, male students would lose their concentration and

wither academically. Unused to the strain of advanced study and the pressure of examinations, female students, in turn, would damage themselves mentally and physically, even threatening their reproductive capacity – a problem somehow not associated with the demands of domestic work, for which women were considered naturally suited. As the student editors of the *Queen's Journal* explained, women's 'proper sphere of action is the domestic circle ... her education should be practical, fitting her to govern her household with wisdom and guidance.'

Despite such opinions, the barriers to women's entry fell for a variety of reasons. By the 1880s, high-school girls were frequently outperforming their male classmates, excelling in matriculation examinations, earning scholarships, and thereby exhibiting their academic potential. Universities, too, came to recognize the economic advantages of boosting their enrolments with female students. The cultural refinement that educated women might bring to their middle-class communities also impressed some previous skeptics, as did the example set by American universities, which enrolled women earlier than did their Canadian counterparts. Finally, the dogged persistence of individual women themselves, who refused to be excluded from the world of higher learning, overcame the resistance of some academic traditionalists. Eliza Fitzgerald was denied admission to Toronto's University College only to win a gold medal for Classics at Queen's University in 1884. Elizabeth Smith and three other female students challenged convention by enrolling in the Queen's medical school in 1880, where they were 'tormented' by the sexually provocative comments of one male instructor and some students. Their experience led, first, to their instruction in a separate, female-only medical class and, then, to the establishment of a women's medical college in Kingston in 1883. In the same year, the Ontario Medical College for Women was opened in Toronto, and for its twenty-two-year history specialized in the health needs of women.

This strategy of educating women separately was pursued with special vigour in the 1880s at McGill University, where the terms of a benefactor's bequest compelled the institution to teach men and women in different classes. A college for the exclusive instruction of women was also planned, but the duplication of facilities required by segregated teaching proved unbearably costly, and, by 1916, the practice had virtually ended. Nor had it endured at other Canadian universities. By contrast, a network of women's colleges thrived in the United States, where they were able to draw from a larger pool of private funding than that available in Canada. As Daniel Wilson, president of the University of Toronto, concluded in 1884, the Ontario government rejected the idea of a college for women on the grounds of 'economy ... Co-education is cheap.'

Mixed classes, however, did not lead to gender equality on campus. In the arts, women were discouraged from enrolling in male-dominated programs, such as philosophy and political economy, and were concentrated instead in literature, music, and modern languages. Women who studied science found it almost impossible to forge academic careers in the area. Professional programs such as medicine and law admitted women in some institutions and denied them access, or imposed entry quotas, elsewhere. As late as 1930, women comprised only 1 per cent of Canada's lawyers and 2 per cent of its doctors. Instead, they dominated the fields of nursing, schoolteaching, household science, and librarianship. Because women (including teachers) were normally compelled to leave their jobs once they married, few entered university in the expectation of preparing for full-time or long-term careers.

In extracurricular activities, women also faced special restrictions. They were barred from many student organizations run by men, had minimal access to student publications, and were subjected to especially paternalistic residence rules. Curfew regulations were so severe at Mount Allison in the early twentieth century that the Ladies' College, where women boarded, was known derisively as the 'penitentiary.' Encouraged by parents, universities took responsibility for protecting the virtue of female students, most of whom were living away from home for the first time.

Women's sphere, then, was unmistakably restricted, both within universities and the larger community. Still, as students, they came from relatively advantaged backgrounds and were often able to profit from their academic experiences. Despite the condescension they endured, McGill women, as historian Margaret Gillett reports, 'had a wonderful time.' They coped with discriminatory treatment less by protesting it than by forging their own social bonds. Women-only societies, such as Levana at Queen's and Delta Gamma at Dalhousie, eased the student's transition to university life, allowed her to cultivate new friendships, and were safe outlets for the expression of common concerns.

Motivated by the spirit of evangelicalism, a significant minority of women across the country joined campus branches of the Young Women's Christian Association, which encouraged Bible study, community service, and missionary work. As Diana Pedersen notes, this early manifestation of the 'social gospel' appealed to the idealism of the young, and to their quest for a moral anchor in a world beset by change. That students frequently were the children of clergymen might also have heightened their religious consciousness. Notably, many students attending the two medical colleges for women, mentioned earlier, heeded the 'call to service.' Veronica Strong-Boag's research reveals that 25 of the schools' 146 graduates between 1883 and 1905 became medical missionaries in various British colonies, where they tended to the sick and promoted the cause of British imperialism.

Most women did not pursue such exotic vocations and, in all likelihood, worked briefly, most often in teaching, and then took up residence in middle-class communities. But, in one important respect, they appeared to defy social convention. Studies of Dalhousie by Judith Fingard, and of Queen's by Lynne Marks and Chad Gaffield, show that university women were far less likely to marry than were women in the general population. In the 1880s and 1890s, between 40 and 50 per cent of the university women from these institutions remained single compared with only 10 per cent of their non-university counterparts. Further research into their fate, and that of subsequent generations, would refine our understanding of the university's impact on women's personal lives and vocational destinies.

Given their expected occupational opportunities, and their comparatively privileged place on campus, men had more to gain than did women from attending university. By the end of the century, they could choose from an array of academic programs and social activities that aided their quest for respectability and status in their communities.

The students who attended university between the 1850s and the 1870s were a select group of males whose social standing would be derived from their classical education, their clerical positions, or their professional vocations in medicine and law. College officials and faculty, the vast majority of whom (in English Canada) had been trained in English or Scottish institutions, believed that higher education would best serve society by cultivating leadership skills among this exclusive community of young men. Regulation of their classroom and campus activities was the favoured means for achieving this end. As A.B. McKillop notes, 'all aspects of the students' lives, at whatever college, were governed by strict forms of domestic and intellectual regimentation.' Students who missed class or chapel services would be fined; chronic truancy could lead to expulsion. Victoria College employed a 'Moral and Domestic Governor' to keep students in line, and college 'wardens' at many institutions administered residences with a heavy hand.

While an atmosphere of earnestness infused student life, there were also signs of restlessness that signalled a desire for greater autonomy in an era of social change. Not only would students periodically disrupt the piety of campus life with pranks or outright acts of defiance, but their religious rituals could contribute to incidents of disorder. At a number of Protestant colleges in the Maritimes and Ontario, evangelicalism inspired campus revivals which included passionate displays of religious commitment. Lasting days, or even weeks at a time, conversion rituals consumed the energies of students in search of moral and spiritual meaning. University officials sought to sustain and channel these religious odysseys while controlling the physical excesses they sometimes elicited. Historian Marguerite Van Die describes a prayer meeting at Victoria College in 1853 which 'ended in chaos when a large number of students, whose souls were at [the] time the object of anxious prayer,' invaded the room, darkened it, and injured one of the evangelists.

While some students pursued missionary work on and off campus, by the end of the century other extracurricular outlets absorbed the abundant energies of university youth. Like scholarly life itself, which had become more specialized and secular in its orientation, student culture was influenced by the values of urban and industrial society. Students now could major in different academic subjects and participate in a variety of social activities. Resembling a type of recreational marketplace, a network of some forty student clubs at the University of Toronto (in 1899) offered literary, debating, musical, scientific, athletic, religious, and other cultural programs. Students across the country were publishing their own newspapers or magazines and experimenting with early forms of student government.

Sheer fun was one reason for their involvement in these associations. But student life also served the university's goal of fostering social leadership and the 'culture of professionalism.' Future politicians or successful businessmen might be found among the ranks of distinguished debaters or student councillors. One could strengthen social contacts, or even find a prospective spouse, in the whirl of extracurricular events. Sharing similar backgrounds and aspirations, students' had their awareness of their special place in society reinforced both inside and outside the classroom.

Initiation rituals, for example, which began appearing in the 1880s, inducted freshmen into the exclusive university milieu by first requiring them to pass a variety of endurance 'tests.' Administered by upper-year students, these rites of passage ranged from the good-natured to the humiliating and violent. A Trinity Medical School 'custom' was directed at 'any student of the first year who was bold enough to take a front seat in the [college] amphitheatre.' He would be 'pounced upon by his superiors, some of whom would endeavour to hoist him up to the back benches while others would struggle to keep him down. In this way the poor innocent would almost be torn from limb to limb.' Opposing a ban on such practices, the student newspaper at Mount Allison contended that 'never should a man from a lower class be favoured or allowed the privileges of those above him.'

University officials attempted to intervene when extreme 'hazing' episodes roused protests from parents and community leaders. Annual Hallowe'en marches in Toronto proved especially disruptive when students invaded theatres and interrupted actors' performances. Invariably, in the wake of 'snake parades' through city streets, damage was done to stores, streetcars, and residential property. Still, in response to these episodes, tolerance more than repression governed university actions. Initiation rites, after all, served to socialize new students into the dominant campus culture and to cultivate loyalty to the institution. Initiations also provided a physical outlet for rambunctious males who might otherwise disrupt the campus peace. And however riotous, these episodes were confined to a particular time of year. As historian Keith Walden argues, male students could be permitted temporarily to behave roughly, mock middle-class respectability, and test authority. 'They were not lashing out at detested conditions, only toying with structures maintained by their own class. They turned the city upside down for a night, then quite happily allowed it to settle back to normality.' Indeed, as Queen's principal G.M. Grant learned, the most effective administrators handled disruptive students with a velvet glove, not an iron fist. According to historian Hilda Neatby, Grant concluded that 'it was never wise to insist upon absolute obedience, or to attack long established even if apparently indefensible [campus] traditions. He discovered how to appeal to the students and to impress them with ideals that they could accept – courage, honesty, loyalty, and inexhaustible zeal in any good cause.'

Periodically, confrontations between university administrators and students were more serious than those fuelled by initiation pranks or illicit alcohol consumption. In the late Victorian era, students rarely demanded a voice in university governance; instead they sought a greater margin of autonomy from paternalistic regulations over their social activities. But, in 1895, University College at the University of Toronto was gripped in crisis after James Tucker, the editor of *The Varsity*, the student newspaper, was suspended for criticizing the appointment of historian George Wrong to the university faculty. Tucker claimed that Wrong, the son-in-law of the chancellor of the university, was the beneficiary of nepotism. His charges were publicly supported by William Dale, a Latin professor, who was then fired by President James Loudon. This inspired a mass meeting of students, a boycott of classes, and a royal commission investigation that largely exonerated the university president while criticizing his handling of student grievances. The student 'strike' was one of a series of incidents which led to another royal commission in 1906, and the subsequent reform of the university's governing structure.

This episode aside, campus rebellions were uncommon. Students had more to lose than gain by rousing the wrath of university officials, who could make their own jobs easier by exercising authority judiciously rather than arbitrarily. Convocation ceremonies, in which students enthusiastically participated, confirmed the legitimacy and austere foundations of university culture. Lasting a full three days at McMaster, the event was replete with solemn rituals rooted in the medieval era. Draped in academic robes, marched in unison, accompanied by baroque music, and certified by the esteemed university chancellor, graduating students bore the symbols of privilege and prepared to assume its rewards.

A study by Chad Gaffield, Lynne Marks, and Susan Laskin of the employment experience of students who attended Queen's between 1895 and 1900 signified the value of a university education. Of those whose occupations were known, a total of 70 per cent ultimately worked in the fields of education, health, or the clergy. A further 26 per cent were employed in law, science, commerce, or government. This represented a wider range of occupations than students had anticipated when they entered Queen's, and far greater possibilities – at least for men – than available a half-century earlier. By 1900, the university was heeding the utilitarian demands of the modern world, and so were its students.

6

Schooling in the Industrial Age

Canada's transition to an industrial society was in full swing by the first decade of the twentieth century, and Canadians greeted this development with a combination of enthusiasm and concern. They cherished the promise of wider occupational options, new consumer goods, and higher living standards. But many were troubled by other products of the emerging urban landscape – the crowds, the poverty, the hazardous health conditions, the wayward youth. Some lamented the erosion of rural life itself. Alas, if industrial capitalism were there to stay, could it not be made to function better? And did schooling not have a vital role to play in facilitating this end? Educational reformers thought so, and school boards, classrooms, and playgrounds all felt the impact of their plans and policies. As in the past, the changes introduced were not always consistent with the visions that inspired them, and on the eve of the First World War, important educational battles had yet to be settled.

The continuous growth, productivity, and urban orientation of the Canadian population were unmistakable by the turn of the twentieth century. Between 1901 and 1913, the number of residents grew by 34 per cent, to 7.2 million. Over the same period, the value of industrial production more than doubled. Factory workers in the East consumed the food grown by Western farmers and built the machinery that helped drive the agricultural economy. The factories themselves attracted bountiful investment from bankers and foreign capitalists. Electricity lit up city streets; new rail lines wove their way across the nation; and rudimentary automobiles trudged treacherously along town and country roads.

The intellectual developments confronting educators – highlighted by the emergence of Darwinian science – were thus accompanied by material changes that would impose new pressures on public schooling. Indeed, certain educational theorists had for some time been bemoaning what they viewed as the irrelevance and ineffectiveness of classroom instruction in the modern era. The rigidness of mental discipline theory, the preoccupation with abstract knowledge, and the drudgery of rote learning allegedly conspired to stifle children's imagination, leaving them ill-equipped to navigate their way in a world of change. Schooling, it was argued, would better serve society by responding to the students' need for activity and subject-matter that, in Douglas Lawr and R.D. Gidney's words, 'more closely related to [their] personal experiences and social environment.'

Two European thinkers prominent in the early nineteenth century – Johann Pestalozzi, a Swiss, and Friedrich Froebel, a German – provided proponents of the 'new education' with intellectual armour in their late-nineteenth-century pedagogical campaigns. Influenced himself by Jean-Jacques Rousseau, Pestalozzi stressed the virtue of developing the child's potential 'in accordance with nature.' Students would gain far more from learning 'how to learn' than by accumulating facts; rather than requiring 'blind obedience,' the school should prepare the pupil for 'independent action.' Accessible to all social classes, the classroom should be as secure an environment as the family home, in which the mother's nurturing role was central.

Froebel also believed in the importance of learning by playing and doing, and demonstrated this theory by creating the world's first kindergarten in 1841. His ideas, however, were at the time too radical for those educators in Europe and North America who were wedded to more formalistic and regulatory instructional practices, and who feared the premature schooling of children. One Ontario educator, James L. Hughes, took up the cause of kindergarten in the 1870s, contending that Froebel's views had more currency than ever in the era of mass schooling. For Hughes, kindergarten could introduce the child to group learning by allowing for 'self-activity,' thus providing a 'bridge from the nursery to the school.' From his position as inspector of the city's public schools, he finally persuaded the Toronto Board of Education to fund a kindergarten in 1883. From then, enthusiasm grew, aided by a promotional campaign conducted by the Dominion Educational Association, and by the first decade of the new century, kindergartens were a common feature of public education across the country.

However, the philosophy that had originally inspired the movement was only marginally evident in the kindergarten classroom itself. While parents and educators favoured more active learning than schools conventionally offered, they still wanted structure and regulation, even for the very young. The typical kindergarten, which in Toronto contained between forty and seventy children, ritualistically required them to play, rest, wash, sit, stand, and march in unison. Routine was stressed, spontaneity discouraged. Rather than stimulating Froebelian-type reforms at other grade levels, kindergarten became, as historian Robert Stamp describes it, the 'new bottom rung on the educational ladder,' designed to facilitate the child's transition from 'structured play to structured work.'

Concerns about the appropriate relationship between schooling and work led to other innovations at the turn of the century, including manual training, domestic science, and vocational and technical education. In pre-industrial society, young men had prepared for occupations as skilled artisans – blacksmiths, shoemakers, tailors – by apprenticing for several years with master craftsmen in these trades. The rise of the factory system, through which goods were produced more cheaply and in massive quantities, forced many craftsmen out of business, thus eroding the system of apprenticeship training. Employers, politicians, and school reformers now argued that public education ought to play a more active role in preparing youth for the demands of the industrial age. As a royal commission report on capital and labour concluded in 1889, the contemporary school system, with its heavy academic emphasis, 'unfits the scholar for mechanical life.'

Manual training, which engaged boys in basic wood- and metal-work, was one popular response to the call for more practical schooling. Among its chief advocates were James Hughes, in Ontario, and Alexander MacKay, the supervisor of schools in Halifax, which by 1894 offered manual training in thirty city schools. The national campaign was boosted in 1899 by support from the Macdonald Manual Training Fund, established by the Montreal tobacco manufacturer and philanthropist Sir William Macdonald. Across the country, the fund initially subsidized training centres affiliated with public schools, and by 1914 manual training had become a regular part of the senior elementary curriculum in most urban communities.

The subject appealed both to traditional proponents of 'mental discipline' and to Froebelian reformers who favoured 'hands-on' learning. By facilitating hand–eye coordination, manual training was intended to strengthen those elements of the brain that contributed to orderly, precise, and analytical thinking, qualities considered essential in technical occupations. Manual training also had supposed moral value; by teaching the student to 'control himself in small actions,' it would inhibit his 'passions and desires,' thus discouraging antisocial, even delinquent, behaviour, a growing concern in the modern city. These were lofty expectations for a program that stressed only the most elementary aspects of the mechanical arts, and as historian George Tomkins notes, reformers later lamented the tendency of schools to merely 'tack' the subject onto an 'already overcrowded curriculum.'

Manual training was offered only to boys because they, not girls, were expected ultimately to work in industrial occupations. But women educational reformers contended that schools were equally obligated to address the utilitarian interests of female students. Among the leading champions of domestic science was Adelaide Hoodless, a Hamilton home-maker, whose eighteen-month-old child had died from ingesting impure milk. She devoted herself to improving the physical, mental, and moral health of the community, and she believed that appropriately trained young women were critical to this mission.

One consequence of industrial living was the employment of thousands of female youth in clerical and factory work. Hoodless lamented this trend because it drew women away from the household and interrupted their domestic education. 'The subversion of the natural law,' she claimed, 'which makes man the bread-winner and woman the home-maker, cannot fail to have an injurious effect on social conditions, both morally and physically.' Instructing girls in subjects such as food chemistry, needlework, cooking, and home management, domestic-science courses, she argued, would make mothers and wives more competent, and family life more durable. Schools could enhance the respectability of home-making by giving the subject academic and scientific credibility. Equipped with this status, women's work would then have 'equal consideration with man's work,' and mothers would no longer be 'the drudge of the family.'

By insisting that girls be prepared for and confined to the sphere of household labour, Hoodless clearly shared the gender biases of male educators at the turn of the century.

But by demanding that schools respond to women's interests, which (as we have seen) they were repeatedly reluctant
to do, Hoodless contributed to the reform movement, and
was strongly supported in her efforts by the National Council of Women of Canada. Due in large part to her persistent
campaign, domestic science was first included in the Ontario curriculum in 1904. Alberta introduced it into the
schools in 1912 and, by 1920, British Columbia had established twenty-nine domestic-science centres. In the Roman
Catholic schools of Quebec, the subject was made mandatory in 1921. In that province, as Marta Danylewycz, Nadia
Fahmy-Eid, and Nicole Thivierge explain, the religious
fragmentation of the school system led to a less uniform
introduction of domestic science into the schools than was
the case elsewhere in Canada. Throughout the country, the
curriculum typically focused on cooking and sewing, and
remained far narrower than Hoodless and other reformers
had anticipated.

That efforts to professionalize the study of 'household
science' bore some fruit was indicated by its appearance in
university curricula throughout Canada. Stimulated by the
need for domestic-science teachers, by 1920 degree or di-
ploma programs in the subject were offered at Mount
Allison, the University of Toronto, the Ontario Agricultural
College, Laval, McGill, and the universities of Manitoba and
Alberta. Nathanael Burwash, president of Victoria College
and a strong proponent of home economics, argued that
the Toronto program, introduced in 1902, far from being
merely technical, was as academically rigorous as the other
liberal arts. Before conducting specialized research in
household economy, students were required over four years
to study philosophy, history, economics, modern languages,
literature, and advanced science. Aside from teaching, occupations open to graduates now included the emerging
fields of dietetics, public health, and nursing. The domestic-
and household-science movements therefore simultaneously reinforced female responsibility for the fate of family

life and secured a measure of public acknowledgment for the importance of 'women's' work.

However elevated were the original goals of manual training and domestic science, these basic courses failed to satisfy the demands of the most determined advocates of technical and industrial education. Secondary schools, argued *Industrial Canada*, the journal of the Canadian Manufacturers' Association, ought to play a more direct role in training skilled workers and foremen able 'to direct the practical side of our national industries.' Lobbyists called for curricular provisions that would both deepen students' understanding of technology and train them for specific trades. While some educators worried about the erosion of scholarly values by business and labour-market pressures, prominent school reformers joined the campaign to link education and industrial life. Not only could academic work be augmented by active learning, but working-class children could be better equipped to contribute to national prosperity and social harmony. By 'dignify[ing] manual toil' through vocational instruction, argued J.H. Putman, inspector of Ottawa's public schools, labour strife – a frequent feature of the industrial era – might well be diminished, with workers and capitalists sharing common educational goals. Indeed, major labour organizations, like the Trades and Labour Congress, supported technical schooling, though some unionists feared the prospect of divisive job competition between young vocational-course graduates and older factory workers. What impressed labour leaders more was the opportunity such schooling might offer the industrial worker to 'rise above the routine of ordinary drudgery ... caused by his daily environment.'

In pursuit of such objectives, a number of educational initiatives were taken in the early twentieth century. A technical school was established in Montreal in 1907. In the same year, Nova Scotia passed legislation which led to the opening in Halifax of the Nova Scotia Technical College, where students studied engineering. In addition, as Donald Macleod notes, local technical schools in other communities offered evening classes in subjects such as mechanical and architectural drawing, chemistry, electricity, and surveying. Miners were encouraged to attend new colliers' schools to learn the 'fundamentals' of safe mining. The Hamilton Technical and Art School was built in 1910. One year later, Ontario's Industrial Education Act augured the introduction of a range of programs, including technical departments in secondary schools, two-year general industrial schools, and, by 1914, evening industrial programs in twenty-seven communities. Commissions were established to assess the need for vocational education in the prairies and British Columbia, though major developments in these regions were delayed until the passage of the federal Technical Education Act in 1919 which authorized significant funding for provincially administered technical schooling.

Assessments of the impact of these programs vary. Defenders have pointed both to the diversity vocational education brought to the conventional high-school curriculum and to the democratic consequences of educating working-class children in programs suited to their occupational expectations. Critics, including contemporary historians, have been less generous in their judgments. B. Anne Wood admires the idealism and public-service commitments of reformer J.H. Putman, but believes that he, and educators who shared his 'progressive' philosophy, contributed more to the moral regulation than to the intellectual liberation of vocationally educated students. Stressing the virtues of efficiency, conformity, and compliance, the programs often added little to the technical knowledge students would later gain in factory or office jobs. In British Columbia, adds Timothy Dunn, vocational schooling was designed to promote 'socially efficient citizenship,' and to stream its lower-class students into menial and manual labour. And according to Ivor Goodson and Ian Dowbiggin, those who hoped that vocational education would attain the status of academic learning were bound to be disappointed. Middle-class families sought to segregate their children in programs that would prepare them for professional careers; vocational and technical courses, attended largely by the less advantaged, offered no such possibility. Thus, rather than facilitating interaction and harmony between the middle and working classes, 'reformed' schooling in the early twentieth century both mirrored and perpetuated the problem of social inequality so characteristic of emerging industrial capitalism.

While acknowledging the material and educational disparity between social classes, some historians suggest that schooling enabled 'labouring' youth to exercise more control over their fate than implied by the above interpretations. John Bullen notes both the increasing school-participation rates and the growth in working-class occupations at the turn of the century, and submits that 'if education did not provide workers' children with opportunities for upward mobility, it at least offered them lateral mobility in the form of a greater number of occupational choices within their own class.' Adelaide Hoodless may have lamented the presence of females in the labour force, but, as Jane Gaskell contends, commercial and vocational studies provided young women with an alternative 'to the existing elitist and male-dominated curriculum,' and directed them to 'new roles involving paid labour.' In a study of Hamilton working-class youth, Craig Heron demonstrates the selective and unanticipated ways this group used public schooling in the early twentieth century. When jobs were plentiful, high school enrolments dropped; as employment opportunities fell, school registrations rose, an attendance pattern that indeed raises questions about the practical value of the education these youth were receiving. Additional community and case-studies of vocational schooling ought to shed more light on this challenging subject. Did students receive genuinely useful and high-quality instruction, or, for want of occupational alternatives, were they merely biding their time in tedious classes conducted by moralizing instructors? Experiences may well have differed from city to city. What seems evident at this stage is that the collaboration of schooling and industry, built on reformers' grand expectations, was something less than a panacea, educationally or economically.

The reformers' interest in applied industrial education should not obscure their profound concern for rural schooling and agricultural studies. Indeed, the gradual transition to urban living, replete with its bleak factory conditions, its noisy commercial bustle, and its competitive, materialistic aura was itself a source of anxiety in some social and intellectual circles. For many Canadians, the country's history and identity were tied irrevocably to its rural roots. In its most exalted form, the countryside was portrayed as the citadel of unequalled natural beauty; honest, invigorating labour; and righteous family values. City children, without exposure to the purifying tonic of country air or the richness of agricultural life, risked growing up without benefit of the greatest bounty Canada had to offer. Congested urban communities, argued critics, were unhealthy and soulless, and inferior places to rear or educate the nation's youth. At the very least, according to this cultural vision, aspects of the rural experience should be included in the school curriculum.

This, in any event, was the view of James Robertson, the Dominion agricultural and dairying commissioner, who, at the turn of the century, convinced philanthropist Sir William Macdonald to fund a practical agricultural program in Canadian elementary schools. The Macdonald Rural School Fund supported school gardens, where children were shown how to plant seeds, rotate crops, and protect them from insects and disease. As historian Neil Sutherland notes, the program, which took root in every province, blended three educational ideas: 'nature study, manual training for rural pupils, and agricultural education for elementary pupils.' Quebec, for example, where the spirit of agricultural revivalism was especially strong, offered (in 1912) gardening programs in 234 schools situated in thirty-five counties.

The campaign to preserve rural ideals in an urbanizing world culminated in 1913 with the passage of the federal Agricultural Instruction Act, which allocated $10 million over the next decade for rural education projects. Provinces spent their share of the money in different ways. Prince Edward Island's government offered a summer course in agriculture at Prince of Wales College, and paid bonuses to teachers who created school gardens. British Columbia hired a provincial director of agricultural education who oversaw both the school gardening program and agricultural courses in high schools. Students undoubtedly enjoyed the break that outdoor activities provided from traditional academic study, but, as Sutherland observes, the results were not uniformly positive: 'Some teachers did only barely enough to collect their grants, provincial governments were slow in adapting courses to local conditions, [and] frequent changes of teachers broke the continuity of the work.'

The challenge of preserving Canada's rural heritage was compounded by the special problems of country schools themselves. The fluctuation of rural-school enrolments, the inferior qualifications of the teachers compared with their urban counterparts, and the unsatisfactory adaptation of curricula to local agricultural needs frustrated both farmers' associations and educational authorities. Consolidation of rural schools into larger units was one proposed solution supported by several provincial governments and by the (Sir William) Macdonald Consolidated School Project. As Neil Sutherland notes, by the outbreak of the First World

War, Manitoba and Alberta were the most enthusiastic prac-
titioners of school consolidation. But in central and eastern
Canada, there was more resistance. Rural communities,
bound to the tradition of the community-based, one-room
schoolhouse, often resented having to send their children
long distances to larger, less personal institutions. Despite
limited educational facilities, sceptical rural families mistrusted provincial officials who told them that consolidated
schooling would provide better-quality instruction at lower
costs. Children feared the loss of such treasured traditions
as the annual Christmas concert, which was the social highlight of the school year. For decades, controversy around
the status of the schools seethed, a poignant example of the
contest between the forces of centralization and local control. The one-room school was not phased out until in the
1960s.

More consensus greeted the introduction of agricultural
education at the college and university level. Degree programs in agricultural studies, stimulated by western expansion, were an early and important part of the curricula of
the universities of Manitoba, Saskatchewan, and Alberta.
The Ontario Agricultural College had been in existence
since 1874, and, in Quebec, Macdonald College, specializ-
ing in agricultural education, was opened in 1907. In
French Canada, new initiatives were taken at Collège Ste-
Anne-de-la-Pocatière and at l'Institut Agricole d'Oka. The
major comparable development in the Maritimes was the
establishment in 1905 of the Nova Scotia College of Agriculture, at Truro. Specialized and sophisticated, the research
and training programs at the higher-educational level
achieved more concrete and enduring results than did agricultural courses in elementary and secondary schools, conceived, as they often were, in the spirit of nostalgia and
romanticism.

The advance of urban, industrial life affected children in yet another facet of their development, according to educational reformers. It subjected them to a more sedentary lifestyle, and deprived them of adequate exercise, a problem less likely to affect rural youth whose farm-based routines were more physically demanding. While physical-education instruction was not unknown in schools before the 1890s, it was generally conducted in a perfunctory way and occupied minimal space in the academic curriculum. Educators stressing the importance of the harmonious development of mind and body had convinced school boards in some jurisdictions to teach calisthenics. In Halifax, for example, as historian Steven McNutt reports, a Sergeant-Major Bailey was hired in 1887 to instruct teachers in these exercises, and in the early 1890s, the Swedish system of calisthenics was being taught to both males and females in city schools. A manual, *Physical Drill for Public Schools*, outlined routines designed to develop limbs and muscles with the aid of dumb-bells. Elsewhere in Canada, there were periodic attempts to emulate the ideals of British 'athleticism' by teaching 'manly' games to schoolboys. Cadet training, too, replete with military-type drills, was offered intermittently in public and private schools. Throughout the country, however, such programs before the turn of the century were selectively, not uniformly, introduced.

A number of influences then combined to raise the profile of school-based physical education. A leading factor, notes historian Morris Mott, was the growing public awareness that 'too many children ... were physically unhealthy.' Epidemics of diphtheria and tuberculosis periodically erupted and spread quickly through poorly ventilated homes and school buildings. Physical exercise, preferably outdoors, was one recommended antidote to these conditions. Indeed, in an era when social-Darwinist thinkers, like the British writer Herbert Spencer, were widely cited, many educators accepted his contention that only the healthiest and fittest of the human species would survive. 'To be a good animal is the first requisite to success in life,' he wrote, 'and to be a nation of good animals is the first condition to national prosperity.' That children were now in schools in such large numbers made it possible to reach them efficiently and at a young age with programs intended to foster appropriate physical development.

Related to concerns about the health of the population was the contention that Canada was at risk because its birth rate, especially among those of Anglo-Saxon origin, was falling at the turn of the century. In light of the influx of European immigrants, fears were expressed – consistent with the racist hereditarian views that informed immigration policy itself – that the country would suffer 'racial degeneration' if its reproductive capacity were not improved. Physically active, able-bodied youth would, it was hoped, eventually help solve this problem. At the same time, British and Canadian games could serve as agents of cultural socialization. If compelled to play games such as soccer and baseball, the children of immigrants might begin 'to see the world in a "Canadian" way, and to appreciate "Canadian" skills and qualities.' As D.S. Woods, the first dean of education at the University of Manitoba, argued (1913), play 'leads to the heart of the foreign child as readily as [to that of] the British born.'

The proper place of games and sports in the lives of Canadian girls, however, was less clearly prescribed. While acknowledging that young females would benefit from some degree of organized physical training, most educators were persuaded that the range of such activities should be more restricted than those open to their male classmates. For the sake of their own health – and that of the nation – women ought to be active, but not to the point of overexertion, a condition which, supposedly, could damage their reproductive organs. Like James L. Hughes, many educators believed that the 'competitive spirit' arose naturally in boys, whereas girls, lacking such drive, were inclined to gentler activities such as 'games of chance, of cards ... and table games.' But where they showed 'interest and zeal,' they should be permitted to participate in the 'milder games of the boys.' Baseball, lawn tennis, and calisthenics were typical of girls' athletics in school. New competitive sports, such as basketball, were also popular, but, for their 'protection,' girls were subjected to special rules compelling them to play the game at a moderate pace. As historian Helen Lenskyj observes, educational authorities wanted nothing – in the academic or extracurricular spheres – to interfere with women's 'nest-building' function.

Yet a further stimulus to physical education for boys was the prospect of war involving Britain and its colonies. Indeed, Canadian troops had been sent to South Africa to help Britain crush the Boer Rebellion in 1899, and this event encouraged the growth of the cadet movement in Canadian schools. By 1900, cadet corps had been formed in thirty-three Ontario schools, and, by 1906, all male students in Halifax academies and high schools were obliged to join a cadet troop. In 1907, the federal Department of Militia provided drill instruction to Canadian teachers, who, once certified, could earn up to $100 a year more in salary. Then, in 1909, the Strathcona Trust, a private foundation, provided $500,000 to Canadian schools for general physical training, military drill, and rifle shooting. Administered through provincial education offices, the program was expected to inculcate discipline, morality, and the spirit of military preparedness among its male participants. Imbued with such qualities, Canadian youth, it was argued, would contribute to the safety both of city streets, and (if necessary) of the British Empire. Women's activities, though supported by the fund, were marginalized, in part because girls were not permitted to become cadets. According to Lenskyj, their participation was generally confined to 'joyless, formal calisthenics.' In the fall of 1914, any frivolity associated with school games ended as the real war began.

Physical education was one instrument used to address the health needs of Canadian youth, a task that proponents of the 'new education' considered vital. A more direct and effective approach involved regulations requiring the clean-up of school buildings, and the employment of medical personnel to inspect and inoculate schoolchildren. The need for such efforts seemed unmistakable. In 1883, the new Ontario Board of Health cited the 'very unsanitary conditions' of many Ontario schoolrooms; continuing neglect would only compound the problem of 'contagious and infectious diseases.' A smallpox epidemic in 1885 killed more than 3,000 people in Montreal. In 1897, there were numerous complaints about the health conditions of Victoria's schools. And, as Neil Sutherland notes, 'in rural areas the battle against filth continued to be an unremitting one.' The Ontario Board of Health noted in the 1880s that the death rate from diphtheria and typhoid was higher in rural districts than in cities. As late as 1918, a survey of Saskatchewan teachers reported the pervasive presence of 'impure water supplies' and 'dirty' privies in provincial schools. Frequently, seepage from outhouses contaminated the well water. Contrary to the contention of agrarian idealists, country living evidently did not guarantee the good health of children.

Facing such challenges, government and school authorities began taking concerted action at the turn of the century. Initiatives elsewhere had already set positive examples. In the wake of a diphtheria epidemic, the city of Boston established the first North American health-inspection program in 1894, followed soon after by Philadelphia, Chicago, and New York. Montreal introduced 'regular and systematic' school inspections in Canada in 1906, as did Sydney, Nova Scotia, one year later. By 1910, several other cities, including Toronto, Winnipeg, and Vancouver, were doing the same. Over the next several years, Toronto's efforts were the most expansive. In 1914, the city's School Health Department had on staff a chief medical officer, twenty-one physicians working as part-time medical inspectors, several dentists, and thirty-seven full-time school nurses. The nurses, who were the linchpins of the inspection system, examined children every two weeks, as did a physician four times a year. The nurses also visited the homes of working-class and immigrant families, where at times they found children in need of medical attention. They lectured parents, usually mothers, not only on appropriate health-care practices, but also on topics such as child rearing, temperance, and home decorating. As historian Kari Dehli suggests, the nurses' sometimes condescending manner could incur the resentment and defiance of the families they visited. Lina Rogers, Toronto's first school health nurse, appointed in 1910, reported that, 'not infrequently, the parents are prejudiced against the nurse before they ever see her, for they conceive the idea that she is interfering with their authority over their children.'

Indeed, while most parents and school authorities favoured the inspection and immunization of their children, there were pockets of resistance to these and other intrusive state-sanctioned practices. New medical treatments were not always trusted by sceptical patients who had witnessed or endured the application of too many ineffective remedies for various maladies. Cost-conscious school authorities themselves often delayed immunizing children until epidemics of smallpox or diphtheria had already broken out, thus minimizing the inoculations' preventative impact. Though recommended by local officials, and provably effective in the past, regular vaccinations were avoided almost entirely in some communities. Even by 1920, according to Neil Sutherland, Saskatchewan health officials reported that 'very few children of school age' had been vaccinated.

The 'reform' movement at the end of the century entailed other forms of government intervention into the lives of individual citizens that met with general but not universal approval. Not only was compulsory-schooling legislation extended and strengthened, but truancy officers were now being used to round up 'missing' students. Child-protection legislation, such as that passed in Ontario in 1893, permitted welfare authorities to remove abused or delinquent children from family homes and place them in the charge of Children's Aid Societies. Many of these youth, in Ontario and elsewhere, were assigned to reformatories and industrial schools, where they were subjected to harsh forms of discipline, and engaged in 'skills' training programs of questionable utility. While theoretical distinctions were made among the needs of 'delinquent,' 'neglected,' and 'abandoned' children, in practice these institutions generally treated incarcerated youth in similarly severe ways. In 1908, federal legislation, the Juvenile Delinquents Act, criminalized the anti-social behaviour of children ages seven to sixteen by charging and trying them in juvenile court. Middle-class advocates believed that such regulations were essential for the health, safety, and moral improvement of urban industrial society. Those most frequently affected by the application of these laws – the poor and their children – did not always agree.

The 'new education' movement was built on ideas that were both novel and traditional. As enrolments swelled, attention to the 'practicalities' of community life – vocationalism, physical training, public health – imposed unprecedented demands on public schooling, augmenting its conventional academic role. In the clamorous world of industrial capitalism, educators were expected to prepare not only a literate, but a disciplined, employable, and productive workforce. Proponents of child-centred learning looked for schools, in the spirit of reform, to cultivate deliberately the student's individuality. But, more often than not, the classroom, bolstered by new laws and larger educational bureaucracies, emphasized, as in the past, the virtues of standardization and uniformity. Also consistent with earlier precedents was the channelling of women and working-class youth into educational streams that opened some new vocational doors without challenging the privileged occupational status of middle- and upper-class males. Canadian schooling had clearly changed by the early twentieth century at a pace that followed, and seldom surpassed, the transformation of Canadian society itself.

Conclusion

Between 1800 and 1914, Canadian society and its school systems were forged, populated, expanded, and reformed. Educational change was not conceived or carried out in a vacuum. In important ways, it reflected the values and the social structures of the communities in which schools were situated. When the circumstances and expectations of the population altered, educational institutions were almost invariably affected. The process of change, however, was usually gradual and seldom free of controversy. Schooling was, and is, a source of acute public concern. When families choose, or are compelled, to share guardianship of their children with teachers and school bureaucracies, they want to have confidence – and they not always do – in the wisdom of educators. To expand the scope of public education in the nineteenth and early twentieth centuries, school promoters required both visions and strategies. They were motivated by ideals and constrained by political and economic realities. The changes they wrought were enormous; still, the policies they implemented rarely achieved everything they promised. Along with intelligence and passion, reformers had one other common trait: they expected schools to do too much. At various times, education was assigned a principal role in advancing the progress, righteousness, morality, patriotism, unity, security, and prosperity of Canadian society.

In frontier communities of the early nineteenth century, families, preoccupied with survival, had relatively little time for formal schooling. Yet, as historians have persuasively argued, the eclectic mix of private and public initiatives revealed considerable interest in the possibility of regular tuition – here was a foundation upon which public schooling might be built. So, too, was the enthusiasm shown for formal education by an array of Christian immigrants who, in the first instance, organized their own schools, and, later, with varying degrees of activism, supported state funding of primary education. Both in the denominationally based school systems of Quebec and Newfoundland, and in the non-sectarian public schools of Ontario and the Maritime provinces, 'Christian' themes and values were propagated in the mid to late nineteenth century.

Other motives also fuelled the expansion of public education. Middle-class citizens, gradually rising to prominence in business and politics in pre-industrial Canada, believed that a prosperous and productive society required a population that was orderly, loyal, and respectful of the growing authority of the state. Playing the role of institutional missionaries, schools could serve society by cultivating appropriate attitudes among students. This was considered particularly vital in the case of immigrant working-class youth whose conspicuous presence affronted middle-class sensibilities. With respect to Native peoples, blacks, and, later, European immigrants, the attempts by schools to reshape values and beliefs according to Anglo-Saxon traditions and norms were especially intense – and suspect, both in theory and in practice.

The intentions of society's leaders aside, ordinary Canadians had their own reasons for favouring state-funded education. Not only would 'free' schooling afford their children the opportunity to obtain an education, but the actual rewards of extended classroom instruction seemed more and more evident. 'Scholars' earned respectability in their communities; literacy could well open occupational

doors, especially amid the decline of apprenticeship training; in an uncertain economy, rural youth with educational
credentials might better equip themselves for the future;
indeed, being suitably 'modern' in a more secular, techno-
logically changing world appeared to require the experience of formal education.

Assembling the school system, however, was a formidable
challenge, and it could not have been accomplished without the employment of thousands of female teachers. But
Victorian society looked askance at 'career' women. Even as
communities both hired females and taught them in larger
numbers, schools marginalized their role by paying instructors less than men, and by restricting the subjects that girls
could study. While the academic options and employment
opportunities of women grew at the turn of the century, the ·
goal of gender equality was seldom articulated, let alone
achieved. Even as they modernized, schools helped keep
alive the popular belief in the centrality of women's domestic role.

Schools and universities were deeply influenced by the
intellectual currents and economic pressures associated
with the rise of industrial capitalism. Darwinian science
hastened the secularization of university culture, and the
demands of industry and the professions spawned a more
utilitarian curriculum at the secondary- and post-secondary-
school levels. Manual training, domestic science, and vocational education together highlighted two important
elements of public schooling in the early twentieth century:
its concern with students' character, including both their
mental and their physical development, and its tendency to
channel youth into particular academic streams according
to their gender and social class. All children now obtained
more schooling than had earlier generations, but both educational and economic privileges still flowed more fully to
those from higher social strata.

These common educational patterns should not obscure
the distinctive features of local and provincial school sys-

tems. For reasons related to the unique religious, linguistic, ethnic, and economic characteristics of Canada's regions, provincial laws governing public funding, separate schooling, compulsory attendance, and university development were introduced at different times and in different ways. So, too, the degree of community involvement in school affairs, and of popular resistance to bureaucratic initiatives, varied from place to place. That schools were subjected to provincial, not federal, authority added to the Canadian educational patchwork, particularly in comparison with the more uniform approaches of other countries.

Despite these forces of diffusion, Canadian school systems, on the eve of the First World War, had much in common and grappled with similar challenges. They looked for more efficient ways to improve and measure students' academic performance. They sought, with as yet uneven results, to respond to the needs of the marketplace. They were obliged to teach more students than ever, and were embroiled in controversy around questions of linguistic and minority rights. They were expected to enrich students' minds, perfect their bodies, and attend to their health. More, perhaps, than any other institution, the school was assigned the job of ensuring the child's transition to a productive, rewarding adulthood. Decades later, these demands, and the conflicting responses they induced, persisted. Over the course of the twentieth century, the promises of schools and the scope of their social responsibilities would not diminish.

References

'General' sources include national and provincial studies, anthologies, and collections of documents that are cited throughout this book. Selected references specific to each chapter are listed subsequently.

General

Barman, Jean, Neil Sutherland, and J. Donald. Wilson, eds. *Children, Teachers and Schools in the History of British Columbia.* Calgary, 1995

del C. Bruno-Jofré, Rosa, ed. *Issues in the History of Education in Manitoba: From the Construction of the Common Schools to the Politics of Voices.* Lewiston, 1993

Dumont, Micheline. *Girls' Schooling in Quebec, 1639–1960.* Ottawa, 1990

Gidney R.D., and W.P.J. Millar. *Inventing Secondary Education: The Rise of the High School in Nineteenth-Century Ontario.* Montreal, 1990

Houston, Susan E., and Alison Prentice. *Schooling and Scholars in Nineteenth-Century Ontario.* Toronto, 1988

Katz, Michael B., and Paul H. Mattingly, eds. *Education and Social Change: Themes from Ontario's Past.* New York, 1975

Lawr, Douglas, and Robert Gidney, eds. *Educating Canadians: A Documentary History of Public Education.* Toronto, 1973

Magnuson, Roger. *A Brief History of Quebec Education: From New France to Parti Québécois.* Montreal, 1980

Phillips, C.E. *The Development of Education in Canada.* Toronto, 1957

Prentice, Alison L., and Susan E. Houston, eds. *Family, School and Society in Nineteenth-Century Canada.* Toronto, 1975

Sheehan, Nancy M., J. Donald Wilson, and David C. Jones. *Schools in the West: Essays in Canadian Educational History.* Calgary, 1986

Stamp, Robert. *The Schools of Ontario, 1876–1976.* Toronto, 1982

Tomkins, George S. *A Common Countenance: Stability and Change in the Canadian Curriculum.* Toronto, 1986

Wilson, J.D., Robert M. Stamp, and Louis-Philippe Audet, eds. *Canadian Education: A History.* Scarborough, Ont., 1970

For a detailed discussion and list of recent writings on the history of Canadian education, see Paul Axelrod, 'Historical Writing and Canadian Education from the 1970s to the 1990s,' *History of Education Quarterly* 36/1 (Spring 1996), 20–38. The journal *Historical Studies in Education* is a particularly important source of Canadian material; it also publishes a regular bibliography of Canadian educational history.

Chapter 1   Schooling and the Community

Bumstead, J.M. *The Peoples of Canada: A Pre-Confederation History.* Toronto, 1992

Dufour, Andrée. 'Diversité institutionelle et fréquentation scolaire dans l'Île de Montréal en 1825 et en 1835.' *Revue d'histoire de l'Amérique française* 41/4 (Spring 1988), 507–35

Errington, Jane. 'Ladies and Schoolmistresses: Educating Women in Early Nineteenth-Century Upper Canada.' *Historical Studies in Education* 6/1 (1994), 71–96

Fahmy-Eid, Nadia. 'L'Éducation des filles chez les Ursulines de Québec sous le Régime français.' In *Maîtresses de maison, maîtresses d'école: Femmes, famille et éducation dans l'histoire du*

Québec, ed. Nadia Fahmy-Eid and Micheline Dumont. Montreal, 1983

Gauvreau, Michael. *The Evangelical Century: College and Creed in English Canada from the Great Revival to the Great Depression*, ch. 1. Montreal, 1991

Gidney, R.D. 'Elementary Education in Upper Canada: A Reassessment.' In *Education and Social Change: Themes from Ontario's Past*, ed. Michael B. Katz and Paul H. Mattingly. New York, 1975

Gidney, R.D., and W.P.J. Millar. *Inventing Secondary Education: The Rise of the High School in Nineteenth-Century Ontario*. Montreal, 1990

Greer, Allan. 'The Sunday Schools of Upper Canada.' *Ontario History* 67 (September 1975), 169–84

Houston, Susan E., and Alison Prentice. *Schooling and Scholars in Nineteenth-Century Ontario*. Toronto, 1988

Jaenen, Cornelius. 'Education for Francization: The Case of New France in the Seventeenth Century.' In *Indian Education in Canada*, vol. 1, ed. Jean Barman, Yvonne Hébert, and Don McCaskill. Vancouver, 1986

Keane, Patrick. 'A Study of Early Problems and Policies in Adult Education: The Halifax Mechanics' Institute.' Histoire s*ociale/ Social History* 8 (November 1975), 255–74

Lawr, Douglas, and Robert Gidney, eds. *Educating Canadians: A Documentary History of Public Education*. Toronto, 1973

McCann, Phillip. 'The Politics of Denominational Education in the Nineteenth Century in Newfoundland.' In *The Vexed Question: Denominational Education in a Secular Age*, ed. William A. McKim. St John's, 1988

Magnuson, Roger. *Education in New France*. Montreal, 1992

Phillips, C.E. *The Development of Education in Canada*. Toronto, 1957

Prentice, Alison L., and Susan E. Houston, eds. *Family, School and Society in Nineteenth-Century Canada*. Toronto, 1975

Smaller, Harry. 'Teachers and Schools in Early Ontario.' *Ontario History* 85/4 (December 1993), 291–308

Tennyson, Brian D., ed. 'Schooldays, Schooldays ... Cocagne
Academy in the 1840s.' *Acadiensis* 5/2 (Spring 1976), 132–7

Tomkins, George S. *A Common Countenance: Stability and Change
in the Canadian Curriculum.* Toronto, 1986

Wilson, J. Donald, Robert M. Stamp, and Louis-Philippe Audet,
eds. *Canadian Education: A History.* Scarborough, Ont., 1970

Wynn, Graeme. 'On the Margins of Empire, 1760–1840.' In *The
Illustrated History of Canada*, ed. Craig Brown. Toronto, 1987

Chapter 2   Building the Educational State

Ariès, Philippe. *Centuries of Childhood.* New York, 1962

Barman, Jean. 'The Emergence of Educational Structures in
Nineteenth-Century British Columbia.' in *Children, Teachers,
and Schools in the History of British Columbia*, ed. Jean Barman,
Neil Sutherland, and J. Donald Wilson. Calgary, 1995

Cross, Michael, and Greg Kealey. 'Introduction.' In *Canada's Age
of Industry, 1849–1896*, ed. M. Cross and G. Kealey. Toronto,
1982

Curtis, Bruce. *Building the Educational State: Canada West,
1836–1871.* London, Ont., 1988

– *True Government by Choice Men? Inspection, Education, and State
Formation in Canada West.* Toronto, 1992

Fleming, Thomas. '"Our Boys in the Field": School Inspectors,
Superintendents, and the Changing Character of School
Leadership in British Columbia.' In *Schools in the West: Essays in
Canadian Educational History*, ed. Nancy M. Sheehan, J. Donald
Wilson, and David C. Jones. Calgary, 1986

Gaffield, Chad. 'Children, Schooling and Family Reproduction
in Nineteenth-Century Ontario.' *Canadian Historical Review*
72/2 (June 1991), 157–91

Gidney R.D., and W.P.J. Millar. 'From Voluntarism to State
Schooling: The Creation of the Public School System in
Ontario.' *Canadian Historical Review* 66/4 (December 1985),
443–73

Houston, Susan E. 'Politics, Schools, and Social Change in
Upper Canada.' In *Education and Social Change: Themes from*

Ontario's Past, ed. Michael B. Katz and Paul H. Mattingly. New York, 1975

Houston, Susan E., and Alison Prentice. *Schooling and Scholars in Nineteenth-Century Ontario.* Toronto, 1988

Manzer, Ronald. *Public Schools and Political Ideas: Canadian Educational Policy in Historical Perspective.* Toronto, 1994

Parr, Joy. 'Introduction.' In *Childhood and Family in Canadian History,* ed. J. Parr. Toronto, 1982

Pollock, Linda A. *Forgotten Children: Parent–Child Relations from 1500 to 1900.* Cambridge, 1983

Robertson, Ian Ross. 'Reform, Literacy and the Lease: The Prince Edward Island Free Education Act of 1852.' *Acadiensis* 20/1 (Autumn 1990), 42–71

Ross, Peter N. 'The Free School Controversy in Toronto, 1848–1852.' In *Education and Social Change: Themes from Ontario's Past,* ed. Michael B. Katz and Paul H. Mattingly. New York, 1975

Shahar, Shulamith. *Childhood in the Middle Ages.* London, 1992

Wynn, Graeme. 'On the Margins of Empire, 1760–1840.' In *The Illustrated History of Canada,* ed. Craig Brown. Toronto, 1987

Chapter 3 Teachers and Students

Alexander, David. 'Literacy and Economic Development in Nineteenth Century Newfoundland.' *Acadiensis* 10/1 (Autumn 1980), 3–34

Barman, Jean. *Growing Up British in British Columbia: Boys in Private Schools.* Vancouver, 1984

Bérard, Robert. 'Moral Education in Nova Scotia, 1880–1920.' *Acadiensis* 14/1 (Autumn 1984), 49–63

Cochrane, Jean. *The One-Room School in Canada.* Toronto, 1981

Danylewycz, Marta. *Taking the Veil: An Alternative to Marriage, Motherhood and Spinsterhood in Quebec, 1840–1920.* Toronto, 1987

Danylewycz, Marta, and Alison Prentice. 'Teachers' Work: Changing Patterns and Perceptions in the Emerging School Systems of Nineteenth- and Early Twentieth-Century Central Canada.' *Labour/Le Travail* 17 (Spring 1986), 59–82

Darroch, Gordon, and Lee Soltow. *Property and Inequality in Victorian Toronto: Structural Patterns and Cultural Communities in the 1871 Census*, ch. 4. Toronto, 1994

Davey, Ian. 'The Rhythm of Work and the Rhythm of School.' In *Egerton Ryerson and His Times*, ed. Neil McDonald and Alf Chaiton. Toronto, 1978

Gaffield, Chad, and Gérard Bouchard. 'Literacy, Schooling, and Family Reproduction in Rural Ontario and Quebec.' *Historical Studies in Education* 1/2 (Fall 1989), 201–18

Gidney, R.D., and W.P.J. Millar. *Inventing Secondary Education: The Rise of the High School in Nineteenth-Century Ontario.* Montreal, 1990

Gossage, Carolyn. *A Question of Privilege: Canada's Independent Schools.* Toronto, 1977

Graff, Harvey. *The Literacy Myth: Literacy and Social Structure in the Nineteenth-Century City.* New York, 1979

Greer, Allan. 'The Pattern of Literacy in Quebec, 1774–1889.' *Histoire sociale/Social History* 11 (November 1978), 393–435

Guildford, Janet. '"Separate Spheres": The Feminization of Public School Teaching in Nova Scotia, 1838–1880.' *Acadiensis* 22/1 (Autumn 1992), 44–65

Harrigan, Patrick. 'The Schooling of Boys and Girls in Canada.' *Journal of Social History* 23/4 (Summer 1990), 803–16

Houston, Susan E., and Alison Prentice. *Schooling and Scholars in Nineteenth-Century Ontario.* Toronto, 1988

Jackson, Nancy S., and Jane S. Gaskell. 'White-Collar Vocationalism: The Rise of Commercial Education in Ontario and British Columbia, 1870–1920.' In *Gender and Education in Ontario*, ed. Ruby Heap and Alison Prentice. Toronto, 1991

McCann, Phillip. *Schooling in a Fishing Society: Education and Economic Conditions in Newfoundland and Labrador.* St John's, 1994

Magnuson, Roger. *A Brief History of Quebec Education: From New France to Parti Québécois.* Montreal, 1980

Phillips, C.E. *The Development of Education in Canada.* Toronto, 1957

Prentice, Alison. '"Like Friendly Atoms in Chemistry?" Women

and Men at Normal School in Mid-Nineteenth-Century
Toronto.' In *Old Ontario: Essays in Honour of J.M.S. Careless,*
ed. David Keane and Colin Read. Toronto, 1990
Selles, Johanna M. *Methodists and Women's Education in Ontario,
1836–1925.* Montreal, 1996
Stamp, Robert. 'Empire Days in the Schools of Ontario: The
Training of Young Imperialists.' *Journal of Canadian Studies* 8/3
(August 1973), 32–42
– *The Schools of Ontario, 1876–1976.* Toronto, 1982
Tomkins, George S. *A Common Countenance: Stability and Change
in the Canadian Curriculum.* Toronto, 1986
Walker, Bernal E. 'The High School Program in Alberta During
the Territorial Period, 1889–1905.' In *Shaping the Schools of the
Canadian West,* ed. David C. Jones, Nancy M. Sheehan, and
Robert M. Stamp. Calgary, 1979
Van Brummelen, Harro. 'Shifting Perspectives: Early British
Columbia Textbooks from 1872 to 1925.' In *Schools in the West:
Essays in Canadian Educational History,* ed. Nancy M. Sheehan,
J. Donald Wilson, and David C. Jones. Calgary, 1986
Whiteley, Marilyn Färdig. 'Annie Leake's Occupation:
Develoment of a Schooling Career, 1858–1886.' *Historical
Studies in Education* 4/1 (1992), 97–112

Chapter 4   Race and Culture

Barber, Marilyn J. 'Canadianization through the Schools of the
Prairie Provinces before World War I: The Attitudes and Aims
of the English-Speaking Majority.' In *Ethnic Canadians: Culture
and Education,* ed. Martin L. Kovacs. Regina, 1978
Barman, Jean. 'Schooled for Inequality: The Education of
British Columbia Aboriginal Children.' In *Children, Teachers
and Schools in the History of British Columbia.* ed. Jean Barman,
Neil Sutherland, and J. Donald Wilson. Calgary, 1995
– 'Separate and Unequal: Indian and White Girls at All Hallows
School, 1884–1920.' In *Indian Education in Canada,* vol. 1, ed.
Jean Barman, Yvonne Hébert, and Don McCaskill. Vancouver,
1986

Bennett, Paul. 'Little Worlds: The Forging of Social Identities in Ontario's Protestant School Communities and Institutions, 1850–1900.' DEd thesis, University of Toronto, 1990

Cooper, Afua P. 'Black Women and Work in Nineteenth-Century Canada West: Black Woman Teacher Mary Bibb.' In *'We're Rooted Here and They Can't Pull Us Up': Essays in African Canadian Women's History*, coordinated by Peggy Bristow. Toronto, 1994

Friesen, Gerald. *The Canadian Prairies: A History*. Toronto, 1984

Gaffield, Chad. *Language, Schooling and Cultural Conflict: The Origins of the French Language Controversy in Ontario*. Montreal, 1987

Grant, John Webster. *Moon of Wintertime: Missionaries and the Indians of Canada in Encounter since 1534*. Toronto, 1984

Harney, Robert, and Harold Troper. *Immigrants: A Portrait of the Urban Experience*. Toronto, 1975

Hryniuk, Stella M., and Neil G. McDonald. 'The Schooling Experience of Ukrainians in Manitoba, 1896–1916.' In *Schools in the West: Essays in Canadian Educational History*, ed. Nancy Sheehan, J. Donald Wilson, and David C. Jones. Calgary, 1986

Linteau, Paul-André, René Durocher, and Jean-Claude Robert. *Quebec: A History, 1867–1929*. Toronto, 1983

Miller, J.R. 'Owen Glendower, Hotspur, and Canadian Indian Policy.' *Ethnohistory* 37/4 (Fall 1990), 386–415

– *Shingwauk's Vision: A History of Native Residential Schools*. Toronto, 1996

– *Skyscrapers Hide the Heavens: A History of Indian–White Relations in Canada*. Toronto, 1989

Mitchell, Tom. 'Forging a New Protestant Ontario on the Agricultural Frontier: Public Schools in Brandon and the Origins of the Manitoba School Question, 1881–1890.' In *Issues in the History of Education in Manitoba: From the Construction of Common Schools to the Politics of Voices*, ed. Rosa del C. Bruno-Jofré. Lewiston, 1993

Pennacchio, Luigi. 'Toronto's Public Schools and the Assimilation of Foreign Students, 1900–1920.' *Journal of Educational Thought* 20/1 (April 1986), 37–48

Stamp, Robert. *The Schools of Ontario, 1876–1976.* Toronto, 1982

Stanley, Timothy J. 'White Supremacy and the Rhetoric of Educational Indoctrination: A Canadian Case Study.' In *Children, Teachers, and Schools in the History of British Columbia,* ed. Jean Barman, Neil Sutherland, and J. Donald Wilson. Calgary, 1995

Titley, E. Brian. 'Indian Industrial Schools in Western Canada.' In *Schools in the West: Essays in Canadian Educational History,* ed. Nancy Sheehan, J. Donald Wilson, and David C. Jones. Calgary, 1986

Tulchinsky, Gerald. *Taking Root: The Origins of the Canadian Jewish Community.* Toronto, 1992

Wilson, J. Donald. 'No Blanket to Be Worn in School: The Education of Indians in Early 19th Century Ontario.' In *Indian Education in Canada,* vol. 1, ed. Jean Barman, Yvonne Hébert, and Don McCaskill. Vancouver, 1986

Winks, Robin. 'Negro School Segregation in Ontario and Nova Scotia.' *Canadian Historical Review* 50/2 (June 1969), 164–91

Chapter 5   Higher Learning

Axelrod, Paul. 'Higher Education in Canada and the United States: Exploring the Roots of Difference,' *Historical Studies in Education* 7/2 (Fall 1995), 141–76

Fingard, Judith. 'College Career and Community: Dalhousie Coeds, 1881–1921.' In *Youth, University, and Canadian Society: Essays in the Social History of Higher Education,* ed. Paul Axelrod and John G. Reid. Montreal, 1989

Frost, Stanley Brice. *James McGill of Montreal.* Montreal, 1995

Gaffield, Chad, Lynne Marks, and Susan Laskin. 'Student Populations and Graduate Careers: Queen's University, 1895–1900.' In *Youth, University, and Canadian Society: Essays in the Social History of Higher Education,* ed. Paul Axelrod and John G. Reid. Montreal, 1989

Gidney, R.D., and W.P.J. Millar. *Inventing Secondary Education: The Rise of the High School in Nineteenth-Century Ontario.* Montreal, 1990

– *Professional Gentlemen: The Professions in Nineteenth-Century Ontario.* Toronto, 1994

Gillett, Margaret. *We Walked Very Warily: A History of Women at McGill.* Montreal, 1981

Harris, Robin S. *A History of Higher Education in Canada, 1663 to 1960.* Toronto, 1976

Johnston, Charles M. *McMaster University.* Vol. 1: *The Toronto Years.* Toronto, 1976

McKillop, A.B. *Matters of Mind: The University in Ontario, 1791–1951.* Toronto, 1994

Marks, Lynne, and Chad Gaffield. 'Women and Queen's University, 1895–1900: A Little Sphere All Their Own?' *Ontario History* 78/4 (December 1986), 331–50

Neatby, Hilda. *Queen's University: And Not to Yield, 1841–1917*, vol. 1, Montreal, 1978

Pedersen, Diana. '"The Call to Service": The YWCA and Canadian College Women, 1886–1920.' In *Youth, University, and Canadian Society: Essays in the Social History of Higher Education*, ed. Paul Axelrod and John G. Reid. Montreal, 1989

Reid, John G. *Mount Allison University.* Vol. 1: *1843–1914.* Toronto, 1984

Strong-Boag, Veronica. 'Feminism Constrained: The Graduates of Canada's Medical Schools for Women.' In *A Not Unreasonable Claim: Women and Reform in Canada, 1880–1920s*, ed. Linda Kealey Toronto, 1979

Van Die, Marguerite. *An Evangelical Mind: Nathanael Burwash and the Methodist Tradition in Canada, 1839–1918.* Montreal, 1989

Waite, Peter. *The Lives of Dalhousie University*, vol. 1. Montreal, 1994

Walden, Keith. 'Hazes, Hustles, Scraps and Stunts: Initiations at the University of Toronto, 1880–1925.' In *Youth, University, and Canadian Society: Essays in the Social History of Higher Education*, ed. Paul Axelrod and John G. Reid. Montreal, 1989

Chapter 6   Schooling in the Industrial Age

Bullen, John. 'Hidden Workers: Child Labour and the Family

Economy in Late Nineteenth-Century Urban Ontario.'
Labour/Le Travail 18 (Fall 1986), 163–87

Danylewycz, Marta, Nadia Fahmy-Eid, and Nicole Thivierge.
'L'Enseignement ménager et les "home economics" au
Québec et en Ontario au début du 20ᵉ siècle: Une analyse
comparée.' In *An Imperfect Past: Education and Society in Canadian History*, ed. J. Donald Wilson. Vancouver, 1983

Dehli, Kari. 'Health Scouts for the State? School and Public
Health Nurses in Early Twentieth-Century Canada.' *Historical
Studies in Education* 1/2 (Fall 1990), 247–64

– 'They Rule by Sympathy: The Feminization of Pedagogy.'
Canadian Journal of Sociology 12/2 (1994), 195–216

Dunn, Timothy. 'Teaching the Meaning of Work: Vocational
Education in British Columbia.' In *Shaping the Schools of the
Canadian West*, ed. David C. Jones, Nancy M. Sheehan, and
Robert M. Stamp. Calgary, 1979

Gaskell, Jane. 'Constructing Vocationalism: Barbara, Darlene and
Me.' In *Rethinking Vocationalism: Whose Work/Life Is It?*, ed.
Rebecca Priegert Coulter and Ivor F. Goodson. Montreal, 1993

Goodson, Ivor F., and Ian R. Dowbiggin. 'Vocational Education
and School Reform: The Case of the London (Canada)
Technical School, 1900–1930.' *History of Education Review* 20/1,
(1991), 39–60

Heron, Craig. 'The High School and the Household Economy
in Working-Class Hamilton, 1890–1940.' *Historical Studies in
Education* 7/2 (Fall 1995), 217–59

Lawr, Douglas, and R.D. Gidney, eds. *Educating Canadians: A
Documentary History of Public Education.* Toronto, 1973

Lenskyj, Helen. 'Training for "True Womanhood": Physical
Education for Girls in Ontario Schools, 1890–1920.' *Historical
Studies in Education* 1/2 (Fall 1990), 205–24

Macleod, Donald. 'Practicality Ascendant: The Origins and
Establishment of Technical Education in Nova Scotia.'
Acadiensis 15/2 (Spring, 1986), 53–92

McNutt, Steven. 'Shifting Objectives: The Development of Male
Physical Education in Nova Scotia from 1867 to 1913.' *Canadian Journal of the History of Sport* 22/1 (May 1991), 32–51

Mott, Morris. 'Confronting "Modern" Problems through Play:
The Beginning of the Physical Education Movement in
Manitoba's Public Schools, 1900–1915.' In *Schools in the West:
Essays in Canadian Educational History*, ed. Nancy M. Sheehan,
J. Donald Wilson, and David C. Jones. Calgary, 1986
Stamp, Robert. *The Schools of Ontario, 1876–1976*. Toronto, 1982
Sutherland, Neil. *Children in English-Canadian Society, 1880–1920:
Framing the Twentieth-Century Consensus*. Toronto, 1976
Tomkins, George S. *A Common Countenance: Stability and Change
in the Canadian Curriculum*. Toronto, 1986
Wood, B. Anne. *Idealism Transformed: The Making of a Progressive
Educator*. Montreal, 1985

Index